Interviewing and Selecting High Performers

Every Manager's Guide to Effective Interviewing Techniques

Richard H. Beatty

John Wiley & Sons, Inc.

Library of Congress Cataloging in Publication Data:

Beatty, Richard H., 1939–
    Interviewing and selecting high performers: every manager's guide to effective
    interviewing techniques / by Richard H. Beatty
      p. cm.
    Includes bibliographical references.
    ISBN 0-471-59360-5 (cloth).—ISBN 0-471-59359-1 (paper)
    1. Employment interviewing. 2. Employee selection. I. Title.
HF5549.5.I6B388   1994
  658.3' 1124—dc20
                                                  93-23779

10 9

To those who believe
that it is "*people*" who make the *only difference*
between "mediocrity" and "high-performing" organizations.

Preface

*M*anagement is presented with few opportunities to exert greater impact on business strategy and organizational results than in the selection of employees. Putting the right persons in place, who are well qualified and motivated to do the work, clearly can have a significant, positive impact on overall organizational productivity and business results. Yet, frequently this critical management activity gets "the short end of the stick" when it comes to investing the time, resources, and effort necessary to do it particularly well. I hope this book will provide the rationale, motivation, and process to change that.

This is more than just another book on interviewing. It is a book for the manager or human resources professional who wishes to upgrade organizational effectiveness through improved selection and hiring results. Although focusing on the interview process, this book goes well beyond basic, conventional interview techniques to incorporate the broader (and far more important) concept of "employee selection."

Most books on interviewing only teach the reader "how to interview," that is, how to ask good interview questions during the interview discussion. Knowing how to ask questions, in and of itself, does little or nothing to improve hiring results. Instead, what is needed is a totally integrated selection process that incorporates both good interview techniques and good interview design and focuses the interviewer's attention on those selection criteria essential to high performance of the job. That is what this book is about.

The first two chapters present the business justification for investing time and resources in the employee interviewing and selection process. Chapter 1 describes the relationship between people and profitability and establishes the preeminence of people as the resource most critical to organizational profitability. Chapter 2, on the other hand, paints a vivid picture of the substantial cost drain caused by poor employee selection.

A broad overview of modern interview theory and practice is presented as a general framework in Chapter 3. This is followed, in Chapter 4, by a thorough review of 10 basic interviewing techniques (with examples) to help the less experienced interviewer formulate more meaningful interview questions.

In Chapter 5, the reader is introduced to the concept of "high-performance models," a critical element of effective employee selection. Such high-performance models, which are constructed by following the well-defined process presented here, accurately profile the essential qualifications for successful (high) performance of a given position. Without first understanding and defining what a high-performer profile looks like, there is absolutely no basis for selecting productive employees, and the entire selection process is doomed to failure.

Using the high-performance model as the basic yardstick for good selection, Chapter 6 then shows the reader how to design an effective interview. The design process introduced in this chapter makes extensive use of modern, behaviorally based interview techniques coupled with a convenient interview design form at the end of the chapter. The task of interview design is further simplified by Chapter 7, which provides the reader with more than 500 behaviorally-based interview questions (covering 32 categories) for use during the interview design phase.

All the fine points essential to conducting an effective interview discussion are then detailed in Chapter 8, The Interview. Topics covered here include selecting and briefing the interview team, choosing and preparing the interview site, formulating the "candidate sales strategy," greeting the candidate, framing the interview discussion, observation and note taking, and closing the interview.

In Chapter 9, a weighted candidate evaluation form is presented for use in evaluating prospective employment candidates. A sample evaluation form appears at the end of the chapter, and the reader is shown how to use this form effectively in evaluating candidates against the high-performance model, developed earlier in the book. The several advantages of this kind of quantitative evaluation approach are also delineated.

The final chapter, Chapter 10, provides an excellent approach for arriving at the final candidate selection decision. This chapter acquaints the reader with the interview team evaluation form, which summarizes the candidate interview ratings of each interview team member and then serves as the basis for finalizing the employment decision through systematic discussion of interview results. Other topics important to the final selection decision, such as reference checking and employment risk analysis, are also discussed. Following the process outlined in this chapter will eliminate much of the guesswork from the employee selection process.

The integrated, step-by-step selection process outlined in this book should not only improve general interviewing skills but also enable managers to become highly capable in the consistent selection of high-performing personnel to meet the overall staffing needs of their organizations. Consistent management selection of "high performers," over the years, can not only guarantee short-term productivity but will also ensure long-term organizational survival and the strategic success of the enterprise.

Few management decisions impact organizational success more significantly than employee selection. Since it is ultimately people who plan, organize, and control all the other resources of the business, organizational profitability and success, in large part, depend on management's consistent selection of high performers to manage and control these resources.

It is time, then, to take employee selection seriously if our goal is to create high-performing, effective organizations that will survive and excel in a world of increasing domestic and global competition. I hope that this book will serve as a good starting point for such selection.

RICHARD H. BEATTY

West Chester, Pennsylvania

Contents

1 People and Profits: The Forgotten Relationship

*A*merican industry has embarked upon a new era, one that is predicated on an increasing need to truly understand the relationship between systems, processes, resources, and profits. Driven by an ever-increasing competitive market, organizations are now seeking to better understand the relationship between *what* they are doing, *how* they are doing it, and profits. The age of "organizational effectiveness" has arrived!

This is the age of "Total Quality" and "Quantitative Techniques." Driven by the motto "Do it right the first time," organizations are busy using quantitative, statistical techniques to study and understand the key variables that impact overall organizational results. They are looking to unlock the secrets of organizational effectiveness—what it takes to consistently produce a high-quality product at lowest cost. In short, they are closely examining the relationship between organizational resources and profit, and all the variables that affect both.

In the spirit of this movement, this chapter explores the relationship between people and profits. My intent is to demonstrate the critical nature of this relationship and, thereby, motivate readers to commit the necessary time, energy, and resources to become highly proficient in the interviewing and selection of people.

I strongly believe that the most important opportunity that management has to impact organizational profitability is the selection of people! This is far from a hollow claim, and the balance of this chapter is dedicated to establishing indisputable proof of this statement.

By using this chapter to cite overwhelming evidence in support of this premise, I hope that, once and for all, managers will clearly understand the people-profit relationship, and that organizations will correspondingly commit the necessary resources, time, and energy to excel in the interview and selection process. In this time of corporate downsizing with the growing need for managers to do more, faster, better, and with fewer people, there is perhaps no more important skill needed by the modern manager than the ability to effectively interview and select people.

PEOPLE AND PROFITS—"A NEW PERSPECTIVE"

As a starting point in understanding the importance of the people-profit relationship, we first need to examine the relationship between the various resources of an organization and the profits generated by that organization. Next, we will need to examine the relationship between the human resource (people) and other organizational resources in the context of profit generation. In the process, I hope to give you a whole new perspective about the importance of people to organizational profitability, and a renewed commitment and dedication to the importance of human resource selection as a vital factor in driving organizational effectiveness.

THE BUSINESS RESOURCES HIERARCHY

Returning to a basic course in economics that I took several years ago, as I recall, there are five basic resources (represented in Figure 1.1) that comprise any manufacturing enterprise. These are:

1. Capital
2. Raw materials
3. Equipment
4. Technology
5. People

It is how well an organization plans, allocates, and utilizes this combination of resources that determines the organization's success and, ultimately, its profitability.

So, examining and understanding the relationships between these resources should yield some excellent insight about organizational effectiveness and profits. Thus, we will embark on a process that closely examines the relationship between each of these key resources and profit. Having done this, we will then seek to understand the critical factor linking these resources together into a winning combination that drives organizational profitability.

CAPITAL

Following the sequence shown in Figure 1.1 and the process previously outlined for exploring the relationship between organizational resources and profit, the first of the organizational resources we need to examine is "Capital." Capital, as we know, is the financial or dollar investment that an organization makes in its enterprise for the purpose of making a profit.

Then what is the key relationship between capital and profitability? Simply put, if capital is wisely invested and properly controlled, the organization will realize a profit. Conversely, if capital is foolishly invested or improperly controlled, the financial results will be disastrous and the organization will fail (suffer bankruptcy).

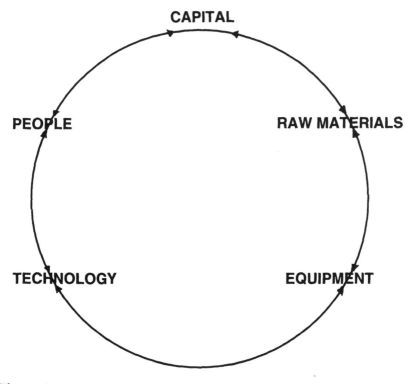

Figure 1.1 *Business Resources*

So then, it is how capital is *planned* and *used* that will determine the profitability of the organization. Simply having lots of capital will not guarantee its financial success or profitability. Likewise, good planning alone, without proper *control* of capital expenditures, will not assure profitability. And finally, excellent control of how dollars are spent will not guarantee profitability unless there is a good plan and the overall investment is a wise one.

Now, the important thing here is that capital neither *plans* itself, nor does it *control* itself. So capital, in and of itself, cannot have any impact whatsoever on organizational profitability without *human intervention*. Instead, it is how *people* plan and control capital that will determine profitability. If employees plan capital well and spend it wisely, in accordance with the plan, the enterprise will thrive and realize financial success. Conversely, if employees make poor investments and spend dollars unwisely, the result is sure to be financial ruin. Let's examine this idea a little more closely.

The first question to consider is, "How is capital *planned?*"

Clearly, capital does not plan itself. Organizations employ financial analysts who are charged with the responsibility for planning the best and most profitable use of capital. It is their principal responsibility to identify and evaluate a host of investment opportunities and to recommend to senior management those opportunities offering the best return on investment (profit) for the firm. So, if the financial analyst does a good job of capital planning, the firm will make money. By contrast, if the financial analyst does a poor job of planning the use of capital, the company can "lose its shirt."

The second question to ask is, "How is capital *controlled?*"

Clearly, capital is incapable of controlling itself. If capital were not controlled and utilized by people, it would simply lay there in a pile in some financial account doing nothing. Once again, without human intervention, capital (in and of itself) is totally incapable of generating organizational profit. On one hand, the wise expenditure and control of capital by employees will ensure profitability, while on the other hand, employee misuse of capital (wasteful and unnecessary spending) will quickly drain company coffers and guarantee financial loss.

Put differently, the capital approval and budget process allocates monies to specific expenditures. People, however, actually spend the money and thus account for the profitability of capital.

Well, here we are then. We've just demonstrated that the key linkage between capital and profitability is really *people.* Without well-qualified, motivated financial analysts, the company cannot expect to plan the best use of capital and experience maximum return. Likewise, without conscientious, trained, and motivated employees, the organization cannot expect its dollars to be well-controlled (spent wisely).

Hence, *people* both *plan* and *control* the use of capital and account for profitability. Why, then, do we spend so much time and effort planning and controlling the use of capital and so little time selecting the people who are responsible for its effective planning and control? An interesting question, isn't it? Perhaps we need to reexamine our priorities.

If our purpose is to maximize organizational profitability through the effective planning and use of capital, then we had better start by hiring those employees best qualified to do so. Effective interviewing and selection of the right employees is the only path to higher profits when it comes to capital as an organizational resource.

RAW MATERIALS

Next on the organizational resource "hit list" is raw materials. Raw materials might be viewed as the chemical and physical ingredients that go into the products we make and sell to generate profit. The type, quality, and cost of these raw materials obviously have a great deal of impact on the financial results of the organization.

If the wrong raw materials are chosen, or if they are of poor quality, the results will be customer dissatisfaction, return of merchandise, cancellation of orders, and financial catastrophe. Likewise if the cost of raw materials is excessive, the results can be loss of sales (due to overpricing) and/or reduced profit margins, both of which will surely lead to profit erosion and eventual destruction of the firm's financial well-being. Finally, improper use of raw materials can result in wastage and drain the company coffers as well.

Thus, proper *selection, use,* and *pricing* of raw materials are critical to organizational profitability. Hardly a startling revelation! Nonetheless, it is an important connection to make if we are going to realize profit improvement through effective use of raw materials as a key organizational resource.

Importantly, raw materials cannot select, use, or price themselves. All these functions are performed by those who manage these material resources. Thus, once again it is *people* who manage and control raw materials, not the resource itself, that accounts for its profitability. Raw materials alone can do nothing to affect profitability. It is how this resource is managed by people that will determine the extent of profit (or loss) to be realized by the organization.

The message is again clear. If we do a good job interviewing and selecting the right people, they will select and manage the organization's raw materials effectively and thus enhance profit generation. To maximize the profitability of raw materials as a business resource, it is therefore imperative that we get the right people in place from the beginning. One of the greatest opportunities to maximize the profitability of this key resource, therefore, rests in the thoroughness of the interview and selection process.

Sometimes, however, we seem to "get the cart before the horse" and spend considerably more time and effort in analyzing our raw materials than we spend in the interview and selection of the people who manage them. What a misguided focus!

EQUIPMENT

This is one of my favorite categories. Perhaps my interest stems from the years I spent as Manager of Technical Employment for a Fortune 100 company, responsible for the selection and hiring of engineering and scientific personnel for the company's research, development, and central engineering functions. In all, I spent over seven years in this capacity, during which time I hired hundreds of technical managers and professionals.

During this experience, I made a key observation early on in my assignment: Most of my engineering clients were so busy doing their engineering work that they seldom had sufficient time to commit to the interview and selection process through which we hired persons to do the work. Almost always, the demands of their technical work took precedence over interviewing and selection. Quite frankly, I always considered this paradoxical! How do you get high-quality, timely engineering results without selecting high-quality engineers? Maybe I missed the point somewhere, but I don't think so.

Anyway, there seems to be a fairly close connection between engineers and equipment. It seems we can't have one without the other.

Equipment, by definition, is the machinery by which work is performed and/or products are made. Generally, equipment falls into two categories: manufacturing equipment and office equipment. Equipment is normally designed to eliminate manual tasks and thus enhance organizational productivity and efficiency. The presumption is that equipment will improve the time and efficiency of the workforce—thus increasing productivity, reducing costs, and generating profits.

The most important thing to understand about equipment is that it neither *designs* nor *operates* itself. Thus equipment, alone, is incapable of creating profit. But, so we don't miss an important point, let's examine this premise a little further.

Equipment cannot design itself. Yet, equipment design is critical to efficiency and productivity. A well-conceived design will improve efficiency, increase productivity, and enhance profits. Conversely, a poor design will impede productivity and

drain profits. So, if equipment designs are to be profit genera-
tors, they must be well designed by engineers.

Again, "profit power" does not reside within the resource.
It is external. It is people who plan and manage the resource. It
is the engineer who delivers either a good design or a bad design. The quality of the engineering, not the equipment itself,
determines whether a given piece of equipment will enhance
organizational profitability or drain profits away.

Thus, the best way to ensure productive, profitable equipment design is to select and hire high-quality engineers, who
are skilled and motivated to get the most out of their design tal-
ents. It's simply too late to think about efficient, competitive
equipment design after you have hired the design engineer. If it
was a poor hire, and the engineer is insufficiently skilled and/
or motivated to produce the results you seek, you've just en-
sured yourself of inferior equipment design and a major drain
on your financial resources.

A well-planned interview and selection process is thus the
best insurance for maximizing equipment design as a profit
producer. However, the job won't get done if you don't invest
the necessary time and effort in the interview and selection
process.

This brings to mind a story that really brings home the
point. It highlights the great paradox I mentioned earlier in this
section of the chapter.

As some of you may be aware, the paper industry is very
capital intensive. A modern paper machine is often the size of
a football field (or larger) and, when fully installed, frequently
has a price tag exceeding $200 million. It is not uncommon for
a paper company to take a year or two, spend several million
dollars, and send a team of engineers halfway around the world
in search of the best paper-making technology and equipment
to meet the project objective.

Yet, the great paradox is that the same company will spend all of a half hour selecting the project manager to oversee the project. Then, two years later and $200 million dollars lighter, the company puzzles over why the machine isn't performing up to expectations. Since the machine didn't design, select, or install itself, I hardly think this is a machine problem. Do you?

Far more suspect are the skills, qualifications, and/or motivation of the engineering staff that did the work! In short, this is not an *engineering* problem—it is a *human resources* problem. The likely culprit was an ill-conceived interview and selection process that lacked sufficient understanding of the knowledge and skills required for successful project results. Chances are the wrong people were selected—resulting in a rather painful and costly mistake!

Well, we can't leave the resource category of equipment without examining the factors of operation and maintenance, and their impact on profitability. Not only does equipment not design itself, but it doesn't operate or maintain itself either. Hence, good equipment design alone doesn't guarantee profitability without effective operation and maintenance. Thus, once again, we trace the relationship between business resources and profits back to the human element.

It is people performing as *operators* who run equipment. If they are well-selected, trained, and motivated, they will tend to run equipment efficiently. By contrast, if they are poorly selected, trained, or motivated, they will lack the skills and desire to be effective operators. The result will be inefficiency, lost productivity, and reduced profits. Conversely, carefully selected personnel who are knowledgeable and motivated will tend to make excellent machine operators. Thus, if you wish to improve machine operations and enhance the profitability of your production process, a good place to start is with the interview and selection process used to choose operating personnel.

Finally, equipment does not maintain itself. It is the *maintenance personnel* who service and maintain equipment. A properly selected, skilled maintenance staff will go a long way toward ensuring that equipment is properly maintained, that machine downtime is minimized, that repair and replacement costs are reduced, and that the equipment is capable of running at optimal performance level at all times. Once again, therefore, *people* rather than *equipment* make a real difference in the profit-generating power of equipment.

It should now be very clear that there is a strong link between equipment and profitability. That link is the *human element.* It is people who determine whether or not equipment, as a resource, contributes profit to the organization or not. It is people who *design, install, start up, operate,* and *maintain* equipment. How well they do these things will determine the extent to which equipment will contribute cash to the firm's bottom line. Equipment, by itself, contributes nothing to organizational effectiveness and profitability. It is simply a business resource that needs to be effectively managed by people if the organization is going to thrive financially.

So, if you are looking for ways to dramatically improve the profits realized from equipment, you can have the most immediate and significant impact by improving your ability to interview and select the people who plan, manage, and control this key business resource.

TECHNOLOGY

Technology, according to *Webster's New Collegiate Dictionary,* is "industrial science"; "applied science"; the "systematic knowledge of industrial arts." I like to think of technology as the application of science to the industrial arts, for the purpose of improving the productivity of machines and people. Hence, technology is an *enabler of productivity.*

Technology, in and of itself, has little or no impact on productivity and organizational profits. It is how people apply technology in the solution of problems that drives improved productivity and profitability. If it is improperly applied, key problems remain unresolved and the organization continues in a less productive state. Where technology is skillfully applied, however, breakthroughs occur, key problems are solved, and the organization advances to a new level of efficiency, productivity, profitability, and competitiveness.

Technology alone accounts for little when it comes to profits. It is how technology is applied by people that has the potential to drive organizational profitability. Once again, we can't ignore the critical relationship between business resources and profits. The profit power of technology rests with the ability of people to apply it. It does not reside within technology itself.

If companies wish to fully realize the profit potential of technology, they must first select technologists who are skilled in applying technology in the solution of those key problems that roadblock productivity and overall organizational effectiveness. Solid interview skills and a well-planned selection process are paramount to selecting the right personnel capable of such technological breakthroughs! Poor interview skills and an inadequate selection process will guarantee technological failure.

PEOPLE—THE REAL CHAMPIONS OF PROFITABILITY

Of all the resources that make up a business enterprise, the most important is people. This is not because it sounds nice to

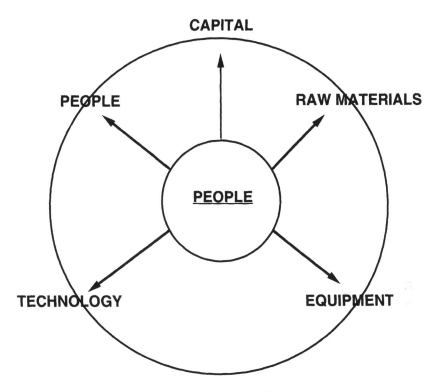

Figure 1.2 *Business Resources Hierarchy*

say this, but because it really is true and can be proven. Consider the following points in support of this statement:

1. People are the *only* business resource with the power to plan and control the other resources of a business.

2. People are the *only* business resource with the power to plan and control their own activities.

3. If an organization does an outstanding job in the selection and motivation of its people, the rest of the organization's resources will tend to be effectively managed and the organization will *prosper.*

4. If an organization does a poor job in the selection and motivation of its employees, the balance of the firm's resources will tend to be poorly managed and the organization will falter and eventually *fail* financially.

5. There is a direct correlation, therefore, between organizational resources, people, and profitability.

6. For these reasons, the interview and selection process is perhaps the single greatest tool that management has to drive organizational effectiveness and profitability.

These principles can best be visualized by reviewing the relational diagram shown in Figure 1.2. The preceding text and this diagram both show that the true key to organizational productivity and profitability rests with human resource selection.

Behind every **business** *problem is a* **human resources** *problem—we either have the wrong person in place* or *the person lacks the necessary skills and/or motivation to get the job done.*

People selection is absolutely critical to effective resource management and organizational profitability.

Managers gearing themselves for stardom during the 1990s and beyond will need to become particularly well skilled in the consistent *selection of high performers*. The times demand this, and the time to learn this skill is now!

CHAPTER 2

The High Cost of Poor Selection

*J*ust what does poor interviewing and selection cost an organization? The answer is "plenty"! Measured as a percentage of labor costs alone, some estimates place the cost of poor hiring and selection at 25 to 50 percent. In other words, high performers are often capable of producing 25 to 50 percent more than their poor-performing counterparts.

Theoretically, then, by consistently hiring high performers, a company could expect to reduce its payroll costs by 25 to 50 percent and still maintain the same level of productivity. This means that a firm having a payroll of $100 million could reasonably expect to lob between $25 million and $50 million off payroll costs by learning how to consistently hire high-performing employees. In this world of intense global competition, what organization couldn't use an extra $25 million to $50 million on its bottom line?

Although the potential for 25 to 50 percent labor cost savings should alone provide excellent motivation for companies to improve interviewing and hiring results, these cost savings can sometimes pale by comparison with the several other categories of poor selection cost that have proven time and again to be major drains on organizational profits. This chapter will fully explore these additional costs of poor selection that so often and unknowingly siphon significant buckets of cash from company coffers.

Many firms feel that poor hiring (that which results in employee termination) has little real cost attached. Unfortunately, nothing could be further from the truth. Such firms often think rather narrowly of only the one or two obvious costs associated with poor selection and fail to come to grips with the far greater hidden costs of negligent employee selection. They think only of the one or two direct, visible costs such as a $20,000 employment agency fee or a $500 classified newspaper advertisement. Unfortunately, these are but minor, insignificant costs when compared with the potential indirect costs that can result from a poor interviewing and selection process.

To understand the magnitude of the cash drain of poor employment selection, we must take a close-up snapshot look at both the *direct* and *indirect* costs associated with this common organizational transgression. Only then will the complete picture come into focus. And, what we will see is likely to come as a real shocker!

Once we focus on the total cost of poor selection, it becomes clear that some really "big bucks" can be gained from improving employee interviewing and selection skills. Further, these significant cost savings can drop directly, and quite noticeably, to the company's bottom line.

DIRECT COSTS

Essentially two categories of direct costs result from poor employee selection: severance costs and replacement costs. To fully appreciate the magnitude of these direct employment costs, we need to examine both expense categories more thoroughly.

Severance Costs

Severance costs are those direct employment separation expenses incurred by a company when involuntarily terminating an employee. These expenses, as normally specified in the firm's severance policy, usually fall into three classifications: severance pay, severance benefits, and outplacement assistance expense.

Severance Pay

Although severance pay policies can vary significantly from company to company, a common standard is for employers to offer one week of severance pay for every year of company service. Many times, this base severance pay is further enhanced for some combination of employee age and/or years of service. A common standard for calculation of such enhanced severance payments seems to be an additional week of severance pay (beyond base severance pay) for every year of service over 15 years with the company. Sometimes an additional week of severance pay is also offered, as part of severance pay policy, for each year of service completed by the employee since attaining the age of 40.

To bring these direct termination costs to life, let's assume the following employee profile:

Age	48 years
Company service	25 years
Annual salary	$75,000
Position	Manufacturing Manager

Based on the previously described standards, the following would be a typical severance pay package for this employee:

Base severance pay	$36,058
Service add on (over 15 years)	14,423
Age add on (over age 40)	11,538
Total Severance Pay	$62,019

Severance Benefits

Besides severance pay, another expensive proposition resulting from employee termination is severance benefits. These benefits, as prescribed by the company's severance policy, normally include the company's continued payment of the cost of insurance premiums (life, disability, medical, and dental insurance) for both the employee and dependents for a specific period (typically coinciding with the length of the severance pay period).

Again, to put these costs into perspective, let's assume that the same manager is separated from the company with the following additional profile:

Marital status	Married, 2 children
Severance pay period	43 weeks
Weekly insurance premiums	$400 (employee and family)

Assume, further, that company severance policy provides that the employer will pay the weekly insurance premiums to cover the employee and dependents for the full severance period of 43 weeks. The result is:

Cost of Severance Benefits = $17,200 ($400 × 43)

Outplacement Assistance

A final direct termination cost associated with discharging a poor performer can be the provision of outplacement consulting support services, a common service now provided to separated employees by many employers. Although the extent and cost of outplacement assistance can vary widely, it is not uncommon for an employer to pay an outplacement consulting firm a flat sum of $6,000 to $10,000 for providing a reasonable level of support services to the employee while he or she goes through the career transition/job search process.

Typically, for a fee of around $6,000, the employee would receive a basic outplacement support program consisting of 2 to 3 days of job search training and 3 to 6 months of support services (office space access, phone usage, secretarial support, and consultant assistance). For purposes of our illustration, we will assume outplacement services are provided to our manufacturing manager by the employer at a cost of $6,000.

We can easily see from our illustration that the direct termination costs associated with our mythical manufacturing manager are mounting rapidly, and they are substantial. A current summary of direct termination costs for separating this employee is as follows:

Severance pay (43 weeks)	$62,019
Severance benefits (43 weeks)	17,200
Outplacement assistance	6,000
Total Severance Costs	$85,219

Besides these direct costs, the company can incur other direct expenses when separating an employee for poor performance. These are what I call replacement costs. Let's now take a few moments to examine this replacement cost category.

Replacement Costs

Replacement costs are those direct costs incurred by the organization in replacing the terminated employee. They fall into the following five key categories:

1. Management interview time.
2. Recruitment advertising.

3. Employment agency or search firm fees.

4. Candidate travel expense.

5. New hire moving expense.

Examination of these costs will reveal that they can add significant economic baggage to the overall organizational expense of poor interviewing and employee selection. Let's take a closer look at these expense items.

Management Interview Time

Simply put, management interview time is the dollar value of the time spent by valuable management personnel and/or professionals in interviewing prospective candidates for a given job. Since such interviewing activities take these individuals away from their normal duties, there is a real cost associated with their time.

In an effort to put this expense item into tangible terms, let's assume the following interview variables, which would be typical requirements for filling a position such as Manufacturing Manager.

1. Average candidates interviewed per hire   4 candidates
2. Average size of interview team   3   managers
3. Average interview time per team
   member   1 hour
4. Average earnings of each team member $85,000/year

You do not have to be a mathematical wizard to quickly calculate the cost of the management interview time required to hire a replacement for our Manufacturing Manager. Based on the preceding interview parameters, total management interview time required is 12 hours. Using a prorated hourly rate of $41 per management hour, total cost of management interview time to hire the manager's replacement would be $492. This does not include the cost of lost productivity while these valuable managers are pulled away from their usual duties to attend to the interview and selection process.

Recruitment Advertising

Recruitment advertising, especially in a major newspaper, is not cheap. A decent-sized classified display advertisement in a major newspaper such as the *New York Times* or *The Wall Street Journal* can easily cost as much as $8,000 to $10,000 per insertion. Lesser known metropolitan papers may charge $3,000 to $4,000 per insertion for a similar advertisement. Thus, we cannot ignore this potential cost, which is frequently incurred by employers who have terminated an unsatisfactory employee.

For the sake of continuing our replacement cost calculation, we will assume that the employer elects not to advertise for our Manufacturing Manager replacement. Instead, the employer decides to use the services of an executive search firm to find this replacement.

Employment Agency and Search Firm Fees

The standard fee charged by the majority of employment agencies and search firms for filling positions paying over $30,000 is 30 percent of total annual compensation (base salary plus bonus). Assuming a base salary of $75,000 plus modest bonus of $7,500, the total fee cost of using a third-party recruiter to replace the manager would be $24,750.

Should the employer use a retained search firm to fill this position, which would not be uncommon for a position at this level, there would also be the added cost of reimbursing the search firm for direct out-of-pocket expenses incurred in carrying out the search assignment. Such reimbursable expenses often include telephone expense, postage expense, and the cost of travel to interview prospective candidates on behalf of the client firm. This expense reimbursement can easily tack another 10 to 15 percent onto the cost of the fee, especially if it involves airfares.

For the sake of our discussion, let's go on the conservative side and assume these reimbursable expenses will cost the company another 10 percent. We will also assume that the company elects to use the services of a retained search firm to fill the position left by the terminated employee. Thus, the added expense would be $2,475, and the full amount paid to the search consultant would total $27,225 (a tidy penalty to pay for poor employee selection)!

Candidate Travel Expense

Continuing with our Manufacturing Manager example, it is also necessary to reimburse employment candidates for their interview travel expenses. This frequently includes transportation expenses (often airfare) and meals and lodging while traveling to and from the interview at the firm's facility. If candidates come long distances, which is often the case for positions at this level, the company must provide for lodging and meals during an overnight stay.

So that we continue to put the real cost of poor selection into perspective, let's assume that we interview a total of four candidates for the position. Let's further assume that two of these candidates are from the local area, and two must fly in from other cities. Although we will not ascribe expenses to the two local candidates, we will assume the company reimburses the following expenses to each of the remaining two candidates, who have flown in at company expense for their employment interviews:

$600 Round-trip airfare
125 1 night's lodging
 35 3 meals
 10 Airport parking fee
  5 Cab fare from hotel to company offices
  5 Tips
$780 Total (Each Candidate)

Using the preceding example, the total travel expense reimbursement for two candidates would be $1,560.

Moving Expenses

A significant factor that companies frequently overlook when considering the cost of poor hiring is moving expense reimbursement. This major expense frequently includes the following items:

1. Cost of house-hunting trip for new employee and spouse.
2. Reimbursement of sale closing costs (old location house).
3. Cost of third-party assistance in sale of old location house.
4. Reimbursement of purchase closing costs (new location house).
5. Shipment of household goods to new location.
6. Final trip of family to new location.
7. Federal tax gross-up for that portion of reimbursable moving expenses reportable as income under IRS rules.

In talking to a former Manager of Corporate Relocation of a Fortune 100 company, I learned that this firm's actual moving expense reimbursement expense per move averaged about

$42,000 in 1990 terms. Adjusting this figure at the rate of 5 percent for annual inflation would yield approximately $50,400 in 1994 dollars.

TOTAL DIRECT COSTS

Now it's time to summarize what we have just discussed. What is the total *direct* cost incurred by the company in terminating and replacing our Manufacturing Manager? Let's look at the following data:

$ 62,019	Severance pay	
17,200	Severance benefits	} Severance Costs
6,000	Outplacement assistance	
492	Management interview time	
27,225	Search firm fee and expenses	
1,560	Candidate travel expense	} Replacement Costs
50,400	Moving expense (1994 dollars)	
$164,896	Total *Direct* Costs	

Amazing! We have just demonstrated that the direct cost of hiring the wrong person as Manufacturing Manager can cost an employer close to $165,000! At this rate, 10 such hires per year could quickly drain over $1½ million from the firm's bottom line.

INDIRECT COSTS

The direct costs of poor selection (both severance and replacement costs) are easily discernible. But, what about the less obvious indirect costs associated with poor interviewing and selection? What are these costs and what is their magnitude?

Although not directly measurable, the indirect costs of poor selection to a company may substantially outweigh the direct costs. Some estimates place these indirect costs at 5 to 10 times the direct costs, or even higher. A quick review of the following list of indirect costs makes this point emphatically. The list underscores that this cost estimate is hardly an exaggeration. To the contrary, it is probably quite conservative.

The Indirect Costs of Poor Selection

1. Lost productivity while terminated employee was employed.
2. Cost of poor decisions made by terminated employee.
3. Lost productivity while awaiting replacement.
4. Cost of training replacement.
5. Lost productivity during training period.
6. Lost credibility of function (if management employee).
7. Lower morale and productivity of subordinates.
8. Poor reputation (in community and industry) as an employer.
9. Increased difficulty (and expense) of recruiting others.
10. Higher unemployment insurance rates.
11. Litigation from negligent hiring/wrongful discharge.

It is quite conceivable that the indirect cost of poor interviewing and selection of a single manufacturing manager could reach the $3/4 million to $1 1/2 million range. In fact, the costs to the company of poor decisions by this manager, during his or her tenure with the firm, could alone well run even into the tens of millions of dollars, if not more. Quite a price to pay for the poor selection of just one individual!

When we consider the relationship of people and profits, so clearly established in Chapter 1, coupled with both the direct and indirect costs of poor selection outlined in this chapter, it should be readily apparent that the selection of people is perhaps management's single most important accountability when it comes to impacting organizational profitability. Few, if any, management decisions can even come close to the total financial impact of employee selection.

Why is it then that so many organizations persist in ignoring this basic axiom? Why is it that they invest so little time, energy, and resources in the interviewing and selection of employees? Why is it that they commit so much more time to the management of the other resources of the business and so little time to the one resource that has the potential to really make or break them—people?

In our increasingly competitive world, which requires managers to do more and more with fewer employees, the ability to consistently hire high-performing workers is becoming a critical skill for survival and success. At the heart of management's ability to hire "high performers" is skill in the interviewing and selection process.

It is my intent in this book to help management to develop interview and selection skills that will enable them to identify and select "high performers" on a regular and consistent basis. In the meantime, it should be painfully obvious that the cost of poor selection can be staggering; this matter of employee selection deserves immediate attention and top billing in the scheme of management's priorities!

3 *Interview Theory and Practice: An Overview*

*M*any employers believe that teaching their managers good interviewing skills will automatically enable them to select better employees and thus improve overall hiring results. Surprisingly, nothing could be further from reality. Improved management interviewing skills will, in and of itself, do little if anything to upgrade overall employment results.

If you find this statement surprising, you are not alone. In fact, you are likely in good company, because most persons would not accept this observation as fact. Its importance, however, rests in distinguishing between the terms interviewing and selection. This critical distinction needs to be drawn if managers are truly to improve their ability to consistently hire high performers—the absolute goal of any good employment process.

INTERVIEWING VERSUS SELECTION—A CRITICAL DISTINCTION

Each year, thousands of U.S. companies waste millions of training dollars on interview training. These companies mistakenly believe that by investing in interview skills training alone, they will improve hiring results. The raw truth, unfortunately, is that interview skills training, by itself, will do little to improve an organization's ability to hire productive workers. Such training programs frequently focus only on interview techniques—ways of phrasing interview questions to elicit more information from employment candidates. All too frequently, such training ignores the very core of an effective selection process—candidate selection criteria (the critical skills and capabilities essential to successful job performance).

Effective hiring and selection processes require managers to be well versed in two critical skill dimensions—interview design and interview techniques. Interview design is the process by which interview techniques (ways of phrasing questions) are applied to candidate selection criteria (the qualifications required for successful job performance) for the purpose of measuring the candidate's qualifications in those areas known to be critical to successful job performance.

Good interview techniques, without a well-planned and focused interview design, will doom the selection process to failure from the start. In the absence of good design, managers will ask the wrong questions and measure the wrong things. Simply put, good interview techniques without good interview design will render the whole interview and selection process useless.

The secret to improved hiring results, therefore, does not rest in interview training alone. For organizations to improve management's ability to hire high performers, they must develop strong management skills in both interview design and interview techniques. Managers need to be taught a totally integrated selection process that effectively integrates the following key elements:

1. Candidate selection criteria.
2. Interview techniques.
3. Interview design.

All three of these elements are critical to consistent selection of high-performing workers—those who will consistently perform their work with an unusually high level of efficiency and productivity.

PURPOSE OF THE INTERVIEW

The purpose of the interview and selection process is for the interviewer to systematically collect evidence of the candidate's ability to perform well in those key areas known to be critical to successful job performance (the candidate selection criteria). Good interviewing techniques allow the interviewer to collect evidence, but good design focuses questioning on those aspects of qualifications essential to effective job performance.

MODERN INTERVIEW THEORY

Modern interview theory subscribes to a single, universal principle that forms the basis for all good interview design. This principle is:

> *Past performance (or behavior) in the same or similar work is the single most reliable predictor of future performance (or behavior) in a given job.*

Thus, if we are going to understand whether or not a candidate is well suited to a given job, we must first start by defining the work to be performed. Then, we must probe the candidate's employment experience to determine how well he or she has performed similar work in the past.

PRINCIPLES OF EFFECTIVE INTERVIEWING

The following are good principles to follow when designing an effective interview and selection process:

1. Interview questions should be "behaviorally based"— they should be designed to examine past or present behavior (or performance) if they are to serve as valid instruments for predicting future performance in the target job.

2. Interview questions must be designed to collect "evidence" of ability to perform those elements critical to successful performance of the target job.

3. Interviewers must base their evaluative judgments on "observable facts," not on feelings and impressions about the candidate's abilities.

BEHAVIORAL INTERVIEWING

The current trend in modern interviewing is toward the use of behavior-based interviewing questions and techniques. The characteristics of behavioral interview design are as follows:

1. Behavior-based interview questions are designed to measure how a person will behave (what the person will do) in a given situation.

2. Situations chosen for exploration of how a person will behave are job relevant and normally fall into three categories:

   a. *Real situations* the candidate must deal with on the job.

    b. *Hypothetical situations,* which are designed to simulate real problems the candidate is likely to encounter in the job.

    c. *Actual situations* that the candidate has encountered resembling those encountered in the job.

3. Situations chosen for interview design should closely reflect actual problems and/or situations the candidate will be required to face in performing the target position for which he or she is being interviewed.

4. A good interview design will incorporate one or more situational scenarios for each key functional area for which the candidate will be accountable.

    (*Note:* The job description can be very useful in identifying these key functional responsibilities.)

5. Beyond the job's functional accountabilities, similar situational scenarios must be developed to reflect special project responsibilities as well.

6. Each situational scenario, incorporated into the interview design, should be designed in the form of a problem to be solved and should measure:

    a. The breadth and depth of specialized knowledge required for effective solution.

    b. The ability to successfully apply this specialized knowledge.

As we review modern interview theory and practices, keep in mind that being trained in interviewing techniques (how to ask questions) is not sufficient to ensure the selection of high performers. The broader issue of effective selection requires that there first be an understanding of the qualifications needed to successfully perform the target position. Without such an understanding, coupled with an effective behavior-based interview design, there will be no valid basis for predicting, with any accuracy, the probability for a successful job and candidate match.

So, for consistent success in selecting high performers, we must pay particular attention to both interview techniques and interview design.

The following chapter will deal with basic interviewing techniques. In later chapters, we will return to the subject of effective interview design.

Basic Interviewing Techniques

*A*s pointed out in Chapter 3, interviewing techniques are methods or ways of asking questions that compel the employment candidate to speak openly and freely about topics the interviewer wishes to probe. Generally, these topics represent key areas of qualification and experience that are essential to successful job performance. The art of effective questioning is at the heart of effective interviewing. How questions are asked will have a lot to do with both the quality and quantity of information extracted from the employment candidate.

This chapter will introduce the reader to basic interview techniques. These will enable the interviewer to design interview questions that will encourage the candidate or interviewee to provide a free flow of relevant information in the areas to be probed during the course of the interview discussion.

For each interview technique, I will first provide a brief definition and then will provide three examples of how you can use this technique to gain considerable information about the topic being explored with the candidate. By providing these definitions, followed by examples of their applications, I hope you will be able to immediately add these basic skills to your interviewing repertoire.

When stripped right down to its basics, interviewing is conversation with a purpose. The purpose of interviewing techniques is to encourage a free-flowing exchange of essential information showing that the candidate has (or does not have) the necessary skills and qualifications to be a high performer in the job for which he or she is being considered. A comprehensive review of these important techniques follows.

OPEN-ENDED QUESTIONS

DEFINITION

An open-ended question is one that requires more than a simple "yes" or "no" answer.

EXAMPLE 1

Close-Ended   Do you like your current job?

Open-Ended   What aspects of your current job do you like most?

EXAMPLE 2

Close-Ended   Does your current job provide opportunities for advancement?

Open-Ended   How would you describe advancement opportunities with your current employer?

EXAMPLE 3

Close-Ended   Do you like your boss?

Open-Ended   What do you like most about your boss?

ONE-STEP PROBE

DEFINITION

The one-step probe is a question designed to collect a limited amount of basic information. These questions begin with the words *who, what, when,* and *where.*

EXAMPLE 1

Who did you work with on the coating project?
What was the outcome of this project?
When was the project completed?
Where was the work done?

EXAMPLE 2

Who most influenced your decision to attend Bucknell University?

What was the deciding factor in your decision?
When did you attend the university?
Where did you go for your graduate education?

EXAMPLE 3

Who did you work for while a project engineer at Loron Company?
What was the nature of your work?
When did you finally leave this position?
Where did you go from there?

TWO-STEP PROBES

DEFINITION

The two-step probe is designed to probe a given area of the candidate's qualifications in greater depth for the purpose of obtaining an increased level of information than provided by the simple one-step probe. Two-step probes begin with the words *how* and *why*.

EXAMPLE 1

How did you come to resign from your position at Telestar Corporation?
Why did you decide to leave?

EXAMPLE 2

How did you solve this difficult problem?
Why did you choose this approach?

EXAMPLE 3

How did you decide to interview with our company?
Why do you have an interest in us?

PAUSE OR SILENCE

DEFINITION

The pause or silence is an interview technique whereby the interviewer simply pauses or remains silent, compelling the employment candidate to talk further on a given topic. It causes the candidate to feel somewhat awkward and nervous, compelling him or her to fill the void with further conversation on the topic currently under discussion.

EXAMPLE 1

Candidate: I just don't know why it happened.

Interviewer: (Silence).

Candidate: I guess I could have been better prepared.

Interviewer: (Silence).

Candidate: Actually, organization is not one of my strong points.

EXAMPLE 2

Candidate: My boss didn't appreciate the amount of work that went into the project.

Interviewer: (Silence).

Candidate: She never really paid much attention to what I was doing.

Interviewer: (Silence).

Candidate: I guess that I should have been more assertive, and attempted to involve her somehow in my work.

EXAMPLE 3

Candidate: No matter what I tried, it didn't seem to matter.

Interviewer: (Silence).

Candidate: I finally went back to my O.D. textbook for some answers.

Interviewer: (Silence).

Candidate: It's amazing how a little research can help. There it was, right before my eyes—an answer to my problem!

THE ECHO

DEFINITION

The echo is an interview technique by which the interviewer simply repeats (or echoes) what the candidate has just said, in the form of a question.

EXAMPLE 1

Candidate:	I was never very fond of him.
Interviewer:	Never fond of him?
Candidate:	Yes, he was known to have a pushy personality.
Interviewer:	Pushy personality?
Candidate:	Yes, I've never enjoyed working with pushy people.

EXAMPLE 2

Candidate:	Jordan was a challenge to work with.
Interviewer:	Challenge to work with?
Candidate:	Yes, he was always late on meeting deadlines.
Interviewer:	Late on deadlines?
Candidate:	Yes, I finally decided to confront him on this issue.

EXAMPLE 3

Candidate:	I had always been very happy at Filmore Corporation.
Interviewer:	Happy?
Candidate:	Yes, I was fortunate to have a boss who recognized my work.
Interviewer:	Recognized your work?
Candidate:	Yes, he was quick to reward his subordinates with recognition for their contributions, and he never tried to claim recognition for their work as if it were his own. He was exceedingly fair and a pleasure to work with.

COMPARISON AND CONTRAST

DEFINITION

With the comparison (or contrast) technique, the interviewer asks the candidate to compare (or contrast) two or more items or events. It is, perhaps, one of the most powerful interview techniques and tends to reward the interviewer with an enormous amount of relevant information.

EXAMPLE 1

Interviewer: How would you compare your job at Belmar
                 Corporation with your position at Blair Industries?

Candidate: Both were interesting jobs, but the position at Blair
                 was far more challenging. We were expected to
                 increase department productivity by 30
                 percent . . .

EXAMPLE 2

Interviewer: Contrast the style of your current boss at Blair
                 Industries with your former boss at Belmar
                 Corporation.

Candidate: Katherine Parker, my current boss at Blair, is an
                 excellent delegator. She provides you with overall
                 direction but allows a great deal of freedom in
                 determining how you will do your work. Steve
                 Johnson, my former boss at Belmar, on the other
                 hand, was not a lot of fun to work for. He had a very
                 controlling style, and he would tend to give detailed
                 instructions as to how he wanted things done.

EXAMPLE 3

Interviewer: Compare the work environment at Blair with the
                 work environment at Belmar. Which did you like
                 most, and why?

Candidate: Blair has an excellent reputation for development of
                 its employees. A lot of emphasis has always been
                 placed on continuous improvement and personal
                 development. Belmar, on the other hand, offered
                 little opportunity for personal development. They
                 lacked the individual focus so important to
                 effectively motivate employees.

THE COMPLIMENT

DEFINITION

The compliment is an interview technique by which the
interviewer offers praise for something the candidate accomplished,

in an effort to encourage the candidate to offer more information on the subject.

To be effective, compliments must be sincere. Candidates easily see through artificial compliments, and this can cause some awkwardness for the interviewer. So, don't offer compliments unless you mean them.

EXAMPLE 1

Candidate:	In my first year as Production Manager, we increased department productivity by more than 30 percent.
Interviewer:	That's quite an increase!
Candidate:	Yes, we accomplished this by systematically focusing on each of our production bottlenecks.

EXAMPLE 2

Candidate:	Our department was awarded 15 patents in the past two years alone.
Interviewer:	That's an impressive accomplishment!
Candidate:	Yes, in fact, 12 of these were in absorbent structures, the area for which my department had primary accountability.

EXAMPLE 3

Candidate:	By the time we finished, all of our customers gave us product orders for a full year in advance.
Interviewer:	Wow, that's really impressive!
Candidate:	Yes, our key competitors were stunned by the inroads we made in the marketplace in such a short time frame.

USE OF EXAMPLES

DEFINITION

With this interview technique, the interviewer asks for examples to support a broad, general statement previously made by the candidate—or to receive more information on how something was accomplished.

EXAMPLE 1

Candidate: I am often described by my boss as one of the most creative persons in our group.

Interviewer: Provide me with some examples of your creativity.

EXAMPLE 2

Candidate: I applied participative management techniques to achieve a greater sense of ownership on the part of department employees.

Interviewer: What are some examples of the techniques you employed?

EXAMPLE 3

Candidate: I have always enjoyed solving some of the more difficult problems.

Interviewer: Give me some examples of some of the challenging problems you have solved.

SITUATIONAL QUESTIONS

DEFINITION

Situational questions are a behavior-based interview technique whereby the interviewer describes a real or hypothetical problem and asks the candidate what he or she would do.

EXAMPLE 1

If you were the Plant Manager of a small, unionized manufacturing facility and personally witnessed an employee steal product, what would you do? Assume there were no other witnesses to the theft.

EXAMPLE 2

You are the only one in the group who understands how to solve the problem, but the boss has a habit of ridiculing you in front of the rest of the department for your intelligence. What would you do?

EXAMPLE 3

You must improve the interview and selection skills of the Accounting Department, but the Corporate Controller doesn't want to take time away from the job to train her managers. What do you do?

SELF-DISCLOSURE

DEFINITION

Self-disclosure is a technique by which the interviewer discloses something of a personal nature about him- or herself to help the candidate feel more comfortable and relaxed about a potentially sensitive topic area.

EXAMPLE 1

None of us is perfect. Each of us has areas in which we can improve. In fact, one of the areas in which I could improve is my organizational skills. What are some areas where you can improve?

EXAMPLE 2

I once had a major blow-out with my boss that almost cost me my job. Give me some examples of some major confrontations that you have had with others, and how did you resolve them?

EXAMPLE 3

I sometimes get frustrated with my boss's style. He has a tendency to criticize his subordinates in front of others. What are some of the things you find particularly frustrating about your boss?

I have now introduced you to 10 basic interview techniques and have provided definitions of each as well as examples of how you can use them to get a candidate to loosen up and share a good deal of information with you. These excellent techniques should serve you well in getting employment candidates to talk more about themselves and provide you with increased data for arriving at an employment decision.

These techniques alone, however, will do little to improve your ability to consistently hire high performers unless you first understand the critical qualifications of the target position that you are filling. They will only enable you to ask better questions and get more information. There is no guarantee that you will be asking the right questions about the right areas— those key areas that are important to successful performance of the target position.

So, interviewing techniques alone are not going to get you where you need to go. They are only part of the answer. To enable you to select high performers, the interview and selection process must first begin by understanding what high performers are. How can you possibly select a high performer without understanding what high performance is? The answer is simple—You can't! This essential factor is the subject of the next chapter.

CHAPTER
5

High-Performance Models

*T*he preceding chapter acquainted you with a number of effective interviewing techniques that will encourage the employment candidate to open up and share relevant information with you. Although these techniques are excellent tools for your interview and selection arsenal, they are but methods to encourage candidate discussion and, in and of themselves, do little to ensure the selection of high-performing employees.

A critical element is missing in our selection equation at this point. Being good at asking questions is one thing, but knowing what to evaluate is quite different. Stated differently, you can be an absolute expert in the use of interviewing techniques, but if you do not have a fundamental understanding of what the critical qualifications are for high performance in the target position (the one for which you are interviewing), there is not much hope for a favorable employment result. Without this vital missing link, you are dooming yourself to failure in perhaps your most important management responsibility—selecting and hiring high performing personnel.

As we have already seen in Chapter 2, the costs associated with poor selection are enormous. As a manager, you are committing yourself (and your employer) to mediocrity or worse when you fail to understand what is essential to high productivity and superior performance in those positions for which you have selection and employment accountability.

Therefore, to ensure optimal selection results, we must begin by defining our selection target—the key qualifications that candidates *must* possess to ensure they are well-equipped to perform the job. Without having defined this target we are shooting in the dark when it comes to selecting high-performing personnel. Without a clear definition of what we are selecting, we might just as well line up candidate names on a dartboard and take a random shot at hitting a winner.

THE HIGH-PERFORMANCE MODEL

Those of us who take management and leadership responsibility seriously, have another option—construction of high-performance (or predictive) models. These are fairly detailed and carefully developed candidate specifications that are used as the basis for employee selection. They reflect the specific knowledge, skills, traits, characteristics, and behaviors that categorize high-performance personnel who can perform the target job productively and efficiently.

By having a known, well-documented, high-performance model in place at the beginning of the selection process, you substantially enhance your odds of selecting someone who will turn out to be the exceptional worker. It will provide you with a far more tangible and reliable basis for measuring prospective candidates and predicting, with greatly improved accuracy, who will be successful and who will not. Hence the interchangeable term: "predictive" model.

Hopefully, you are now aboard and agree on the need to prepare high-performance, predictive models in advance of the interviewing and selection process. But, what are the key elements of the high-performance model process, and how do we go about building a reliable model as the basis for employee selection?

This question is perhaps more easily asked than answered. The rest of this chapter, however, will focus on providing the necessary information.

THE STRATEGIC SELECTION MODEL

Figure 5.1 illustrates a useful model that briefly outlines the steps of a successful employment and selection process. This multidimensional model effectively portrays a systemic, integrated, step-by-step process for candidate selection that focuses on those qualifications essential to successful job performance.

I have dubbed this model the "strategic selection model" due to its focus on the three selection dimensions that are critical to predicting future job performance success—job fit, strategic fit, and cultural fit.

Work Analysis

The logical place to begin our quest for a definition of high performance is with the work itself. We must first have a thorough understanding of the responsibilities of the position.

A good starting point for our analysis of responsibilities is with a copy of the job description. If no job description exists, it is probably an excellent idea to begin by constructing one. In that case, you will need to prepare a comprehensive listing of the key functional responsibilities of the position. Take each of the major functional areas for which the person will be responsible and define the key results that he or she must accomplish in each of these areas to be a complete success in the position.

A fundamental principle to keep in mind when analyzing the job description is that "jobs exist because problems exist." If problems did not exist, there would be no necessity

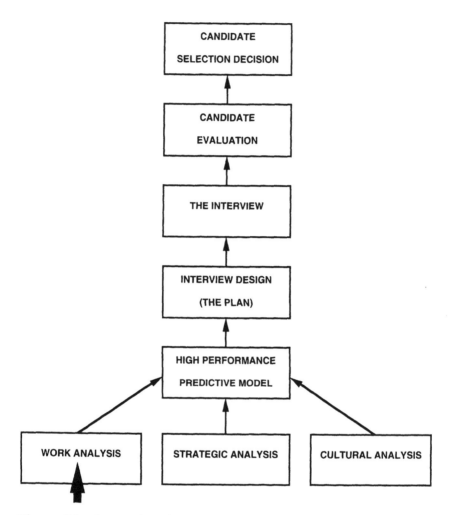

Figure 5.1 *Strategic Selection Model*

to employ anyone. When it comes to work analysis, therefore, identifying the key problems to be solved is at the heart of good selection. After all, the need to solve these problems and achieve the desired results is why we are hiring an individual in the first place.

Proper job analysis involves the following sequence:

1. List each *functional area* for which the position is accountable (each key function either performed or managed).
2. Define the *key results* expected in each area of functional responsibility.
3. Identify the *key problems* (barriers and obstacles) that must be solved to achieve the expected results.
4. Identify the general and specialized *knowledge* needed to successfully solve these problems and realize the required functional objectives of the position.

I have provided the following broad categories of knowledge to further facilitate your thinking about the type of knowledge required by the target position:

1. Concepts	8. Laws
2. Techniques	9. Principles
3. Methods	10. Theories
4. Standards	11. Technology
5. Procedures	12. Equipment
6. Fields	13. Processes
7. Regulations	14. Functions

Figure 5.2 illustrates a way of visualizing this job analysis. You will note that the position can require one or more functional results for each key functional accountability. Each of these expected results then has one or more key problems that the position incumbent will need to solve to achieve that desired result. Then, each key problem is further analyzed to

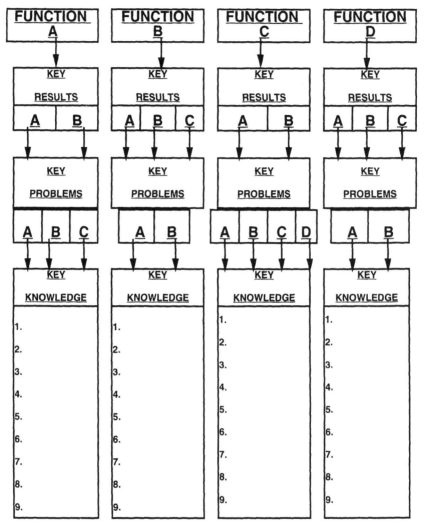

Figure 5.2 *Job Analysis*

ascertain what general and/or specific knowledge is needed to successfully solve it.

Interestingly, as we strip away each layer of the position analysis, from functional responsibility to result to key problem, the final product of the evaluation process is "knowledge." Therefore, when it comes to determining whether or not a given candidate will be capable of performing the job, the interview process needs to zero in on three factors:

1. Knowledge to solve key functional problems.
2. Ability to apply that knowledge.
3. Motivation or desire to solve these key functional problems.

Simply having the required knowledge in a given functional area is not, in itself, a good measurement of whether or not a certain candidate can be a high performer. Rather, you must determine whether the candidate has the ability to apply this knowledge and is motivated to do so.

Most of us have, at one time or another, witnessed the phenomenon of a brilliant PhD scientist who, despite a magnificent academic record, seems to have little ability and/or desire to apply that knowledge to the work at hand. Hence, although qualified technically, this individual has little or no probability of becoming a high performer in the organization. Instead, critical pieces of work go undone, and eventually the company needs to confront the situation by replacing the employee with someone who is both capable and motivated to perform the work.

Conversely, if the candidate has a strong desire to do the work but lacks the requisite knowledge to perform, the results can be equally disastrous. This lack of knowledge will result in incorrect solutions to key problems, wasted resources, and a general deterioration in the quality of organizational results.

So, good interview design (when measuring the candidate's ability to perform the job) must incorporate all three elements:

1. Knowledge.
2. Application of knowledge.
3. Motivation to apply knowledge.

Stated more appropriately, the employment interview needs to focus on answering the following three important questions:

1. Does the applicant possess the critical knowledge needed to solve the key problems that he or she will face in the position?

2. Can the candidate apply this knowledge in the successful solution of these key problems?

3. Is the candidate motivated to apply this knowledge to these problems?

To determine that a particular candidate is going to be productive, all these questions must be answered in the strong affirmative through the "behavioral evidence" collected during the interview process. You must therefore examine past or current behavior in the solution of these or similar functional problems. This factor will need to be the principal focus of your interview design when you prepare to examine those job-related qualifications needed for successful performance in the target position.

Chapter 6 will provide you with some excellent approaches to interview design that will help you thoroughly probe this functional knowledge area, but first we need to conclude development of our high-performance model.

Project Analysis

We have just concluded that portion of work analysis having to do with the ongoing functional accountabilities. The second dimension of job analysis, which is also important to selection of high performers, however, has to do with the project accountabilities of the position.

Besides the ongoing functional responsibilities of a job, most positions also have some additional responsibilities of a short-term, temporary nature. These are the "project accountabilities" of the position. Typically, they are aimed at achieving a one-time solution to a problem (or problems). Once the problem has been solved, the project goes away, and the job incumbent ceases to have further responsibility for this aspect of the work.

It is also quite common for workers to have project accountability for one or more special project assignments. These accountabilities are a very real aspect of the position's overall responsibilities, and employment applicants must be fully capable of successfully executing such assignments if they are going to be productive, high-performance employees.

The process for defining project-related selection criteria, as part of high-performance model development, is almost identical to that used in determining the selection criteria for ongoing functional accountability. Interestingly, the end result of your analysis will once again be key knowledge. But, I am getting ahead of the process—so, let's focus our attention on the project aspects of the job.

Figure 5.3 illustrates the project analysis process. It begins by defining each of the projects for which the candidate will be responsible as an integral part of his or her job performance. Next, specific desired project results are delineated for each project for which the candidate will be responsible. Careful examination of each desired result will again point up that certain key problems will need solutions in realizing project objectives. Finally, further evaluation of these specific problem areas will make it evident that candidates must possess a certain body of knowledge to achieve successful solutions.

As pointed out earlier in this chapter, job knowledge can fall into several broad categories. The following list should help stimulate your thinking on this topic:

1. Concepts
2. Techniques
3. Methods
4. Standards
5. Procedures
6. Fields

7. Regulations	11. Technologies
8. Laws	12. Equipment
9. Principles	13. Processes
10. Regulations	14. Functions

Again, as described earlier with functional accountability, prospective employment candidates will also need to possess the requisite project knowledge, have the ability to apply it, and be motivated to solve these particular problems if there is going to be some reasonable profitability of a good job fit and resultant high performance. Lack of the required knowledge, application ability, or motivation and desire to tackle these key project problems will almost certainly spell performance disaster.

So, as we step back and take an overall view of our high-performance model thus far, these are the principal elements that we have developed:

Work Analysis

1. Functional Analysis

    a. Key ongoing functional responsibilities.

    b. Desired functional results.

    c. Key functional problems requiring solution.

    d. Key functional knowledge required for solution.

2. Project Analysis

    a. Key project responsibilities.

    b. Desired project results.

    c. Key project problems requiring solution.

    d. Key project knowledge required for solution.

Now go to Figure 5.7 (page 79), at the end of the chapter, and complete the work analysis portion of the high-performance, predictive model.

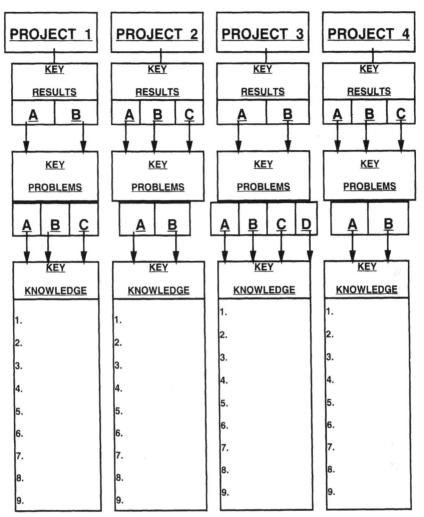

Figure 5.3 *Project Analysis*

STRATEGIC ANALYSIS

So that we do not lose sight of the overall process that we are following, it is a good idea to once again view the strategic selection model (see Figure 5.4). Review of this model shows that the next step in the construction of the high-performance selection model is "strategic analysis."

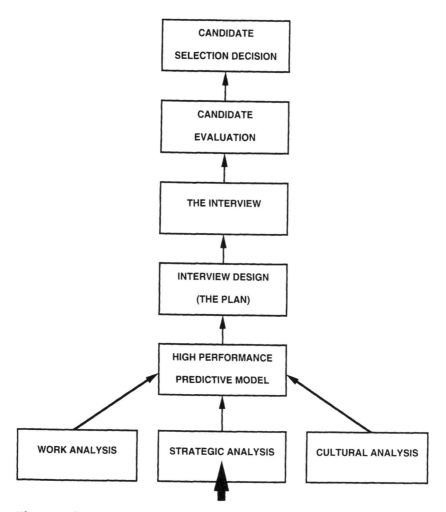

Figure 5.4 *Strategic Selection Model*

Far too often, in the heat of everyday job demands, managers tend to look at the current job (as now performed) without giving much thought to the strategic implications of filling a given position. Unfortunately, this results in selection of employees who may be capable of performing the current position but do not possess the qualifications needed by the organization to fulfill its strategic mission.

The result of such shortsighted selection is to cripple the organization's strategic capability. In the short run, things may work out quite well, but two or three years later (when it is time to drive the required changes to support long-term strategic goals), it is suddenly discovered that the current job incumbent possesses neither the ability nor the motivation to lead the necessary changes. Consequently, the organization must replace this employee with someone who has the credentials and desire to bring about the strategic shifts essential for long-term organizational success.

As pointed out in Chapters 1 and 2, the costs of such shortsighted selection can be enormous. Real costs can often run into the tens of thousands, if not millions, of dollars.

Here again, people selection is one of the few real opportunities that management has to significantly impact business success. By putting in place candidates who are a good "strategic fit," management ensures the organization's survival and the realization of its strategic objectives. Without such qualified employees in place, the cumulative effect is to guarantee eventual strategic paralysis and long-term failure.

Therefore, no high-performance, predictive model can be complete without incorporating business strategy into the employee selection process. For this reason, our strategic selection model shows this as the next step.

A critical dimension of effective employee selection, strategic analysis is a fairly simple and easily understood phenomenon. It is the process of examining business strategy for the purpose of identifying those candidate qualifications essential for successfully performing the strategic responsibilities of a given job. The process can be visualized by reviewing the model depicted in Figure 5.5.

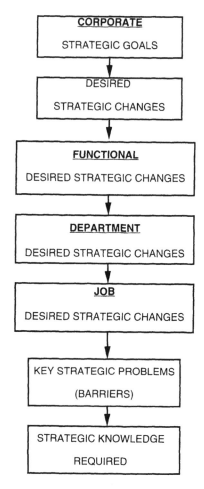

Figure 5.5 *Strategic Analysis Model*

As shown in this model, the process begins by identifying the overall long-term strategic mission and goals of the organization. The specific process steps are as follows:

1. Determine the corporation's long-term strategic goals (its desired future state).

2. Determine the current state of the organization with respect to these corporate long-term goals.

3. Define the strategic changes required by the corporation to transition from its current state to the desired future state.

4. Define what specific strategic changes will now need to be carried out, *at each level* of the organization, to achieve the overall strategic goals of the firm, as follows:

   a. *Functional* strategic changes

   b. *Departmental* strategic changes

   c. *Job* strategic changes

5. Determine what key problems must be solved (or barriers removed) by the target job to bring the desired strategic changes and improvements about.

6. Determine the specific knowledge required by the job incumbent to successfully solve these strategic problems or remove these barriers.

Ironically, by contemplating the significance of this model, it is easy to see how management (if focusing on the strategic requirements of the position) can use the employee selection process to facilitate and aggressively drive the strategic change process. Put differently, by purposely selecting employees who are exceptionally well qualified and motivated to bring about the desired changes, the organization can accelerate these changes and achieve its long-term mission quickly and efficiently, realizing an enormous competitive advantage in the marketplace!

As with work analysis, from the employee selection standpoint, the focus of strategic analysis is on the same basic three factors discussed earlier:

1. Knowledge

2. Application of knowledge

3. Motivation to solve problems

These factors are all critical ingredients of interview design for the selection of high performers. The absence of any one of the three will result in the selection of someone who does not have the ability and/or motivation to assist the organization in realizing its corporate long-term goals—a serious disadvantage for any firm looking to achieve competitive advantage and eventual dominance in the marketplace.

Now, turn to Figure 5.7 (page 83) and complete that section of the high-performance, predictive model that pertains to the strategic dimensions of candidate selection.

Chapter 6 will help you to design effective interview questions for evaluating candidates against this strategic dimension. But now, as confirmed by the strategic selection model (see Figure 5.6), let's continue with development of the final component of the strategic selection model—organizational culture.

Organizational Culture

No high-performance model would ever be complete without defining the cultural dimensions required for employee high performance in a given work environment. By the term "organizational culture," I mean the desired values, beliefs, traits, characteristics, and behaviors that categorize high-performing personnel within the given work environment.

Behavioral scientists have long known that as groups of people associate and work together in an organizational environment, the interaction among the group members will eventually result in the emergence of a central set of organizational values and principles critical to effective performance in the group. The basic core values and beliefs that eventually emerge from this social interaction then begin to serve as the basis for defining such important cultural factors as:

1. Preferred/acceptable business philosophy

2. Preferred/acceptable management philosophy

3. Preferred/acceptable operating style

4. Preferred/acceptable personal style

5. Preferred/acceptable organizational behavior

Those employees who most closely subscribe to the central values, beliefs, and principles of the organization, and demonstrate this through their behavior, are the ones who will

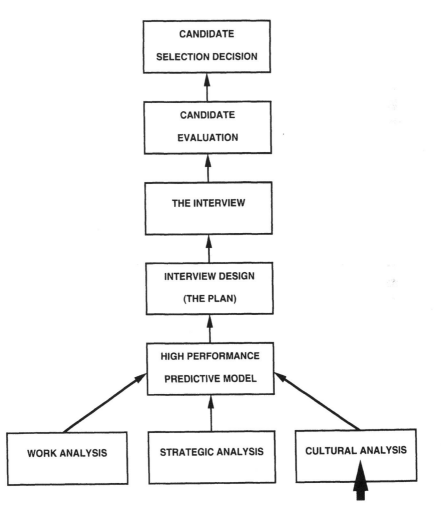

Figure 5.6 *Strategic Selection Model*

receive maximum support from the organization. It will be they who get the organizational backing required for organizational success. They are the fortunate ones who find it easy to sell their ideas to management, secure the resources and capital necessary to carry out their ideas, and secure the backing and encouragement of management along the way. And, when they succeed, it is they who reap the recognition and rewards that accrue to high performers.

On the other hand, we have all witnessed, at one time or another, the certain demise of those who do not fit with the core value and belief system that is central to ensuring performance success in an organization (i.e., the "poor performers").

Since personal values and beliefs formulate the basis for people's principles, and therefore their behavior, those whose personal values and belief systems do not align well with the central, accepted value and belief system of the organization will have difficulty "fitting in." They will not behaviorally exhibit the preferred philosophy and styles encouraged and rewarded by the organization. In such cases, you are likely to hear comments like these:

1. John doesn't understand what is important here—he tends to focus on unimportant things and neglects key job priorities.

2. Mary lacks an appreciation for the big picture—she doesn't have good strategic vision.

3. Bob doesn't seem to fit in with the group—he's not a team player.

4. June has poor interpersonal skills—she is argumentive and inflexible.

5. Bill is just not fitting in with the group—he is quiet, a loner, and seldom contributes.

6. Elaine is a disruptive individual—she is always fighting with others in the group.

7. George has strange ideas—he lacks the vision and focus required by our group.

8. I'd like to terminate Heather—she's just not working out.

The results of lack of alignment with organizational culture are unfortunate but real. Such individuals, although often bright and technically sound, cannot get the basic support they need to be effective in the organization's environment. They have difficulty selling their ideas to others, cannot get management backing, and cannot get the vital resources and/or support needed for successful performance. Hence, the organization virtually renders them "nonproductive," and soon "performance issues" emerge along with eventual management requests for their separation from the company.

Supporting this observation, I conducted a limited survey a few years ago demonstrating that somewhere between 70 and 92 percent of all involuntary professional and managerial "performance" terminations have absolutely nothing to do with technical competence (the technical knowledge and ability to perform the work) and everything to do with cultural incompatibility (the inability to fit with organizational culture). Not a totally surprising statistic for anyone who has spent some time in the field of human resources.

Although such culturally based terminations are often carefully couched in performance terms, the frequent reality is that incompatibility issues, with either the boss or work group, are the real culprits behind the scenes.

Despite management's general willingness to readily concede the great importance of organizational compatibility as a critical factor in successful employee selection, amazingly few organizations even attempt to measure this factor as part of their employee selection process. Instead, the bulk (if not all) of their interview and selection focus is concentrated on "technical fit"—whether the candidate has the specialized knowledge and skills to perform the work.

Sometimes, during evaluation and comparison of finalist candidates for the position, you may hear some vague reference to cultural fit, such as, "I think she would fit in well with our group." Unfortunately, many times this is as sophisticated as it gets.

I have always felt that the key reason management seems to ignore cultural fit in favor of technical fit is not that they don't appreciate the importance of this factor, but that they simply lack a good process for measuring it. In the absence of a good process, this "soft" aspect of selection is the area with which management is least comfortable. Therefore, the tendency is to avoid it in favor of the more tangible, measurable aspects of technical fit.

In any case, it is essential for managers to understand organizational culture if they are to stand a chance of selecting high performers with any kind of consistency. Conversely, failure to select candidates who align well with organizational culture (the core value system, belief system, and general work environment) will build in, and substantially increase, the probability of employee performance failure. Such individuals will simply not get the support and resources required for success, despite their technical competence and ability to perform the work.

By now, I hope you are fully convinced of the need to measure and predict the organizational compatibility of candidates as a prelude to successful selection of high performers. Now all that's missing is a process for accomplishing this.

Organizational Profile

The first step in measuring organizational compatibility is to understand the cultural profile of the target organization. This can be somewhat complex depending on the size of the organization.

Research has shown that in a very large organization, such as Du Pont, IBM, and General Electric, there may be one overlying culture, but within it there can be many different subcultures. In such organizations, successful selection requires definition of the unique subculture within which the individual will actually be working.

For example, in one business unit (e.g., a mature business where growth has topped out and focus is primarily on modest product improvement and marketing strategies designed to capture slightly larger market share), the environment may be more cautious and conservative. Here, minor changes in strategy may result in huge financial impact based simply on the size or scale of the business. Such environments may thus tend to favor individuals who are "careful, thorough, analytical, and cautious" in their decision making.

On the other hand, in another business unit within the same company (e.g., a small greenfield, start-up business in a high-growth market), the organization may be thinly staffed and managers and professionals are required to make quick decisions without the benefit of much advance analysis. Successful employees in such a work environment might well be described as "decisive, intuitive risk takers, able to make fast decisions (despite considerable ambiguity and lack of data)."

The contrast between the requirements of these two organizational cultures begins to make my point about the importance of organizational compatibility. The point is simply this: Employee A, who has been enormously successful in the mature business environment, may be a total failure if transferred to a start-up business culture. In one case, this employee was rewarded as a high performer for being "cautious, careful, and analytical." The same behaviors, however, in a start-up environment, may render the employee totally ineffective. Unable to part with a work style that favors caution and carefully analyzed decision making based on factual analysis, this employee could well fall victim to cultural incompatibility and find him- or herself on the short end of a performance improvement plan and eventual termination from the company.

So, hopefully the importance of my message on "cultural fit" is clear. The same individual with a given set of traits, characteristics, and behaviors can be a "tremendous success" in one work environment and a "total disaster" in another. The answer to this problem has nothing to do with technical competence and everything to do with lack of fit with the culture of the employing organization.

The process of cultural analysis must begin with an understanding (in behavioral terms) of the culture or work environment of the target organization into which the candidate is to be hired. More specifically, it must reflect the immediate work environment (function and department) in which the individual will be working.

Cultural Surveys

The best-known method for establishing a valid profile of the preferred behavioral attributes of a given work environment is through a scientifically based cultural survey. Generally such a survey has two parts:

1. *Psychological Assessment.* The approach used here is to employ various assessment instrumentation to measure the traits, characteristics, tendencies, and behaviors of known high performers along with correlation studies that link these patterns with actual performance evaluation data.

2. *Employee Population Survey.* This technique is normally employed in conjunction with psychological assessment as a further means of validating the observations about high performers. Additionally, it is used to uncover statistically validated performance-related data about the work environment itself.

Generally, such studies are better performed by qualified outside sources having specific expertise in this area. Our firm, Brandywine Consulting Group, Inc. (Malvern, Pennsylvania), has developed expertise in this field and can provide you with meaningful assistance in understanding and documenting the cultural profile of your organization. Should you require additional information on this topic, we can be reached at (215) 429-5125. There are other human resource consulting organizations with expertise in this area as well.

Basic Process

If your firm lacks the resources and/or internal capability to conduct validated studies of your work environment, the following simplified process may prove useful to you. Asking the following questions about both the work environment and high performers should help establish your organization's cultural profile:

Work Environment

1. What adjectives best describe the work environment in which this job functions?

2. What distinguishes this work environment from other work environments (both inside and outside the organization)?

3. What words best describe the type of work performed by this job?

4. What adjectives best describe the environment from the standpoint of how decisions are made by this position?

5. What words best describe the work environment from the standpoint of how resources are allocated to and by this position?

6. What is the behavioral basis for an effective working relationship between this position and other functions with which this position must interface?

7. What is the behavioral basis for effective working relationships between this position and other positions within the same function?

8. What is the role of this position, if any, in determining broad plans and business strategies?

9. How would you categorize the management style and philosophy of the department in which the position is located?

High Performers:

1. Who are the obvious organizational leaders in the immediate work group—those who have been particularly successful?

2. In what ways are these leaders "unique or different" from mediocre or poor performers?

3. How would you describe these leaders in terms of:

   a. Business philosophy.

   b. Management style/philosophy (if managers).

   c. Operating style.

   d. Personal style.

4. What traits, characteristics, and behaviors set these high performers apart from others in the organization?

5. Who are the poor performers in this organizational unit?

6. What do these poor performers have in common?

7. What sets these poor performers apart from others in the organization in terms of:

   a. Business philosophy.

   b. Management style/philosophy (if managers).

   c. Operating style.

   d. Personal style.

8. What traits, characteristics, and behaviors set these poor performers apart from others in the organization?

These questions will yield a great deal of valuable information about the work environment as well as the traits, characteristics, and behaviors required for successful performance in this organizational culture.

Now complete the balance of the high-performance, predictive model (see page 84) using the information gathered during the cultural analysis phase just completed. You will then have an excellent basis for measuring the probability of organizational fit of prospective employment candidates for this position. The profile compiled in Figure 5.7 should provide you with an excellent benchmark against which to compare the personal profiles of interested candidates and greatly improve your ability to select high performers.

USE OF THE PREDICTIVE MODEL

In Chapter 6, we will use the high-performance model constructed here as the basis for effective interview design. Now that we know what high performers "look like" (their profile in terms of knowledge, skills, traits, characteristics, and behaviors), we have a far more reliable basis for interviewing and predicting the probability for successful job performance.

The next chapter will concern itself with interview design. Specifically, now that you have established a reliable "high-performance model," how do you go about designing an effective interview process that will allow you to measure prospective candidates against this model and thereby significantly enhance your ability to consistently select high-performing individuals?

As you will quickly see, the model you have created in this chapter will serve as an excellent basis for such interview design.

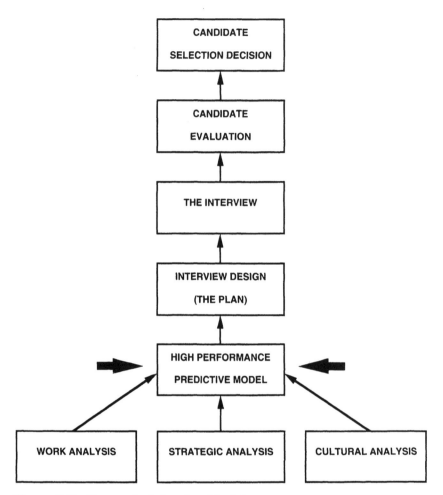

Figure 5.7 *Strategic Selection Model*

High-Performance/Predictive Model

I. WORK ANALYSIS

   A. FUNCTIONAL ACCOUNTABILITY

      1. Functional Result

_____

_____

      Key Problems to Be Solved

_____

_____

_____

      Knowledge Required

_____

_____

_____

_____

      2. Functional Result

_____

_____

      Key Problems to Be Solved

_____

_____

_____

      Knowledge Required

_____

_____

_____

_____

      3. Functional Result

_____

_____

      Key Problems to Be Solved

_____

_____

_____

Figure 5.7 *(continued)*

Knowledge Required

_____

_____

_____

_____

4. Functional Result

_____

_____

_____

Key Problems to Be Solved

_____

_____

_____

Knowledge Required

_____

_____

_____

_____

5. Functional Result

_____

_____

Key Problems to Be Solved

_____

_____

_____

Knowledge Required

_____

_____

_____

_____

6. Functional Result

_____

_____

Figure 5.7   *(continued)*

Key Problems to Be Solved

_____

_____

_____

_____

Knowledge Required

_____

_____

_____

_____

_____

7. Functional Result

_____

_____

Key Problems to Be Solved

_____

_____

_____

_____

Knowledge Required

_____

_____

_____

_____

8. Functional Result

_____

_____

Key Problems to Be Solved

_____

_____

_____

_____

Knowledge Required

_____

_____

_____

_____

Figure 5.7   *(continued)*

B. PROJECT ACCOUNTABILITY

  1. Project Result

    _____

    _____

    Key Problems to Be Solved

    _____

    _____

    _____

    Project Knowledge Required

    _____

    _____

    _____

    _____

  2. Project Result

    _____

    _____

    Key Problems to Be Solved

    _____

    _____

    _____

    Project Knowledge Required

    _____

    _____

    _____

    _____

  3. Project Result

    _____

    _____

    Key Problems to Be Solved

    _____

    _____

    _____

Figure 5.7   *(continued)*

Project Knowledge Required

_____

_____

_____

_____

_____

II. STRATEGIC ANALYSIS

  A. STRATEGIC CHANGE

_____

_____

    Key Problems/Barriers

_____

_____

_____

    Knowledge Required

_____

_____

_____

_____

  B. STRATEGIC CHANGE

_____

_____

    Key Problems/Barriers

_____

_____

_____

    Knowledge Required

_____

_____

_____

_____

  C. STRATEGIC CHANGE

_____

_____

Figure 5.7   *(continued)*

Key Problems/Barriers

_____
_____
_____
_____

Knowledge Required

_____
_____
_____
_____
_____

D. STRATEGIC CHANGE

_____
_____

Key Problems/Barriers

_____
_____
_____
_____

Knowledge Required

_____
_____
_____
_____

III. CULTURAL ANALYSIS
    A. WORK ENVIRONMENT
        1. Descriptors—Work Environment

      _____
      _____
      _____

        2. Descriptors—Type of Work

      _____
      _____
      _____

        3. Descriptors—Decision-Making Process

      _____
      _____
      _____

Figure 5.7 *(continued)*

4. Descriptors—Resource Allocation Process

_____

_____

_____

5. Descriptors—Basis for Effective Working Relationships
   (External Functions)

_____

_____

_____

6. Descriptors—Basis for Effective Working Relationships (within
   function)

_____

_____

_____

7. Descriptors—Type Role in Business Planning and Strategy
   Formulation

_____

_____

_____

_____

8. Descriptors—Management Philosophy and Style (within
   function)

_____

_____

_____

_____

B. HIGH PERFORMERS
   1. Leaders/High Performers—Uniqueness and Distinctiveness

_____

_____

_____

_____

_____

   2. Leaders/High Performers—Business Philosophy

_____

_____

_____

_____

_____

Figure 5.7   *(continued)*

3. Leaders/High Performers—Management Philosophy and Style

_____

_____

_____

_____

_____

4. Leaders/High Performers—Operating Style

_____

_____

_____

_____

_____

5. Leaders/High Performers—Personal Style

_____

_____

_____

_____

_____

6. Leaders/High Performers—Key Traits, Characteristics, and Behaviors

_____

_____

_____

_____

_____

Figure 5.7   *(continued)*

CHAPTER
6

Interview Design

*R*eview of the strategic selection model (see Figure 6.1) confirms that the next step in the interview and selection process is "interview design." Interview design is the process by which interview techniques (ways of phrasing questions) are applied to candidate selection criteria (the high-performance, predictive model) for the purpose of measuring candidate qualifications in those areas critical to successful job performance.

In the preceding chapter, you systematically constructed a high-performance employee selection model through careful analysis of the nature of the work to be done, the strategic goals of the organization, and the organizational climate in which the job is performed. In this chapter, then, we will use the critical employee selection criteria defined by this model to formulate an interview plan and key questions that will provide the behavioral evidence to accurately predict the probability of a candidate's successful job performance in the target position for which we are interviewing.

To accomplish this, we will work right off the high-performance model, designing interview questions to systematically examine candidate capability in each of the critical selection areas defined by the specific components of this predictive model. We have already demonstrated the relevance of these factors to an effective interview and selection process. We will now use them as the basis for actual interview design.

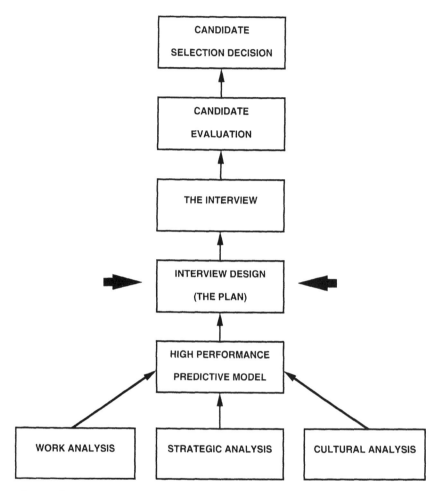

Figure 6.1 *Strategic Selection Model*

MEASURING KNOWLEDGE

As you will recall from the preceding chapter, both work analysis and strategic analysis result in the eventual identification of critical job knowledge required to perform the work of the target position (both the functional and the project work) as well as the knowledge that will be critical to supporting the organization's strategic goals. So, in evaluating prospective employment candidates in both the *work* and *strategic* dimensions, we will need to probe their knowledge in those areas defined by you in the high-performance model as critical to successful job performance.

Additionally, as you may recall, we must evaluate three critical dimensions of knowledge:

1. Existence of the required knowledge
2. Ability to apply this knowledge
3. Motivation to apply this knowledge to the problems that will be encountered in the job

Also, when designing questions to evaluate a candidate's knowledge in a given area, keep in mind that knowledge is acquired in only two ways:

1. *Formal.* (Education and/or training)
2. *Informal.* (Experience)

Both of these dimensions must therefore be thoroughly probed for behavioral evidence of depth and breadth of knowledge in those areas critical to performance of the functional accountabilities, project responsibilities, and strategic requirements of the target position.

But, as already stated, it is not enough to know that the candidate has the required knowledge to perform the job. We must also be able to ascertain, through the interview process, that the candidate can also apply this knowledge to the key problems (both work and strategic related) he or she will actually encounter in the job.

When it comes to measuring a candidate's ability to *apply* this knowledge, I know of only two interview approaches that can effectively measure this quality:

1. Problem simulation
2. Citing of examples

In both cases, these methods will allow you to collect fairly reliable behavioral evidence of both the candidate's knowledge as well as his or her ability to apply that knowledge. Having established the existence of the required knowledge and the ability to apply it, we are then left with the final challenge of measuring the candidate's motivation to apply this knowledge to the kinds of problems he or she will encounter in the job.

Let's start first by gaining some understanding about the two approaches for measuring the knowledge factor—"problem simulation" and "citing examples." We will return to the matter of motivation a little later in the chapter.

Problem Simulation

Problem simulation is an excellent behaviorally based interview technique for probing a candidate's know-how. It allows you to make valid behavioral observations concerning both the existence of required knowledge as well as the ability to apply it.

When using the problem simulation technique, you simply pose real or hypothetical problems and ask the candidate how he or she would go about solving them. This is sometimes referred to as "situational interviewing." The candidate is presented with a problem in the form of a situation and then must provide a solution.

This is an excellent approach to interviewing because it allows you to observe what the candidate will actually do. Thus, it is a behaviorally based technique that enables you to observe, firsthand, how the candidate will attack the problem as well as the likely result. Since current or past behavior is the best known predictor of future behavior, this technique will allow you to use current observation (during the interview) as the basis for predicting how well the candidate will actually perform in the job.

It should be fairly obvious from this discussion, then, that the problems you choose to probe a candidate's knowledge in a given area should simulate as closely as possible the actual problems he or she will encounter in the job for which they are being interviewed. In fact, wherever possible, they should be given actual problems and situations that they will face as job incumbents. This will assure you of a more valid measurement of job-relevant capability and will result in a more accurate prediction of future job performance.

The following, then, are the steps that you should follow when designing this phase (work and strategic knowledge factors) of the interview process.

1. Design carefully selected problems or situations for presentation to the candidate in the interview.

2. Wherever possible, these should reflect actual key problems that the candidate will need to solve in the job itself.

3. The problems or situations chosen must require using the key knowledge needed for successful job performance.

4. After posing these problems to the candidate, the interviewer will be able to make the following important behavioral observations:

   a. Does the candidate demonstrate appropriate depth and breadth of required knowledge?

    b. How well is the candidate able to apply this knowl-
       edge?

    c. How motivated does the candidate appear to be in
       finding a solution?

    d. What is the quality of the solution?

Interestingly, this problem simulation technique will also allow you to make some other behavioral observations while the candidate is tackling the problem. These include:

1. Intellectual capacity

2. Resourcefulness/creativity

3. Quickness of thought process

4. Organizational ability

5. Logic

6. Analytical ability

7. Conceptual ability

8. Thoroughness

Where any of these traits are critical to successful job performance, you will realize an added bonus when using the problem simulation technique.

Now, I would like to focus your attention back to the predictive model you constructed in the preceding chapter. The beauty of constructing a predictive model is that it compels you to identify the key problems (and required knowledge) involved in successful job performance right from the onset. Thus, by returning to the high-performance model at this point, you have a ready-made list of key problems from which to choose in developing your interview design. Further, you know with a great deal of certainty that these are the very problems that the candidate will need to solve to ensure high performance in your target position. Whey then choose any others?

So, your first step in constructing an effective, behaviorally based interview design is to simply extract the "key problems set" from both the *work analysis* and the *strategic analysis* portions of your high-performance model. These problems will be the means of evaluating whether the candidate has the requisite job knowledge, project knowledge, and strategic knowledge to perform the target job at a high level.

You will now want to extract these problems and arrange them by the three appropriate categories (job knowledge, project knowledge, and strategic knowledge) on the interview planner at the end of this chapter (see pages 111–113).

Citing Examples

As mentioned earlier, another good interview design approach to measure candidate knowledge is citing examples. In using this technique, you simply ask the candidate to describe problems (similar to those key problems he or she will need to solve on the job) they have tackled in their current or past jobs.

After requesting that the candidate furnish examples, you will need to ask some probing follow-up questions, as part of your interview design, in order to obtain usable behavioral evidence of the candidate's ability to perform in those areas critical to job success. These probing questions might include:

1. Describe the problem—what was particularly difficult about it?
2. How did you approach the problem?
   a. What approaches did you consider? Why?
   b. What approach did you elect to use? Why?

3. What results were achieved?

   a. Could these results have been improved? How?

   b. Knowing what you now know, what would you have done differently? Why?

Here again, you will want to draw from your previously constructed predictive model to define the key problem areas that need investigation. Doing so will facilitate interview design and keep you focused on designing questions that will probe relevant areas critical to successful performance of the position.

Although it is certainly an effective way of probing candidate knowledge, this technique is a much less desirable (and effective) alternative than the use of *actual* problems the candidate will face in the position. Real problems will be a far more reliable predictor of future job performance. They simply provide a "purer" measurement and, as such, are far less susceptible to candidate manipulation.

Further, actual problems require more spontaneous, real-time responses on the part of the candidate. They will certainly provide you with a much more objective, reliable basis for making behavioral observations about such things as quickness of thought, resourcefulness, creativity, organizational and analytical ability, logic, intellectual capacity, and thoroughness.

Motivation

Now, as promised, we return to this matter of motivation. It is one thing to determine, through good interview design, that the candidate has both the knowledge and the ability to apply that knowledge to the key problems at hand, but what about the motivation actually to do the work (to solve the problems facing them)? Well this one is a little tougher to handle.

First, you can make some observations about the level of motivation when using either the problem-simulation or citing-examples techniques. To do so will require you to be particularly attentive to *how* the candidate responds to the problems you have served up on the interview platter. Observe the general energy and level of excitement as the candidate both contemplates and begins to solve the problem. This will surely provide some behavioral evidence of the candidate's level of interest and motivation for doing the work.

Another, and perhaps more reliable, approach to measuring the candidate's level of motivation is to incorporate a more direct approach into your interview design. Since, as we have already stated earlier, the best predictor of future behavior is current and/or past behavior in the same or similar kind of work, then our design needs to examine the candidate's past work history as the basis for predicting job motivation. The questions we need to have answered are:

1. What type of work has the candidate most enjoyed in the past?
2. What kinds of work has the candidate least enjoyed in the past?
3. Is the work you are offering most like the work the candidate has enjoyed, or most like the work the candidate least enjoyed?
4. What kinds of problems and challenges does the candidate find particularly stimulating?
5. What kinds of problems and challenges does the candidate find least stimulating?
6. Which of the two categories (most stimulating vs. least stimulating) most closely resembles the problems and challenges of the target position?

This kind of comparison should provide you with some pretty good behavioral evidence of the candidate's level of motivation and desire to perform the type of work you have to offer.

Here are some typical questions you will want to include in your interview design for measuring motivation to perform the job in question:

1. As far as technical challenge (problems requiring your solution), which of the jobs that you have held did you find most stimulating?

2. What about this work did you find particularly interesting?

3. Of the positions you have held, which did you find least technically challenging and stimulating?

4. What about this kind of work did you find least satisfying?

5. What types of problems do you most enjoy tackling? Why? Give me some examples of such problems and tell me what you enjoyed about them.

6. What types of problems do you least enjoy tackling? Give me some examples of such problems. What about them did you least enjoy?

In questions 5 and 6, the focus on providing examples forces the candidate to provide concrete, reliable behavioral data based on reaction to past work. There is less likelihood, therefore, that the candidate will attempt to fake the answers given. Thus, your observations are rooted in past behavior, not in what the candidate feels you would like to hear.

Now turn to the end of the chapter (Figure 6.2, page 113) and incorporate your questions for probing job motivation into the appropriate section of the interview planner.

By now, we have pretty much exhausted the topic of measuring both job and strategic knowledge as well as the motivation to apply it. The next step in interview design, as you might expect from the strategic selection model, is the design of interview questions for measuring cultural compatibility.

CULTURAL COMPATIBILITY

Cultural compatibility, as explained in Chapter 5, is an often forgotten but vital dimension of employee selection. Those who do not align well with the culture of the organization will not be empowered by that organization. To the contrary, they will experience great difficulty in fitting in and will be unsuccessful in their bid for the organizational resources and support necessary to successful performance. This lack of general support will render them ineffective and nonproductive in the organizational climate in which they must work.

Therefore, selection of high performers will require you to measure the cultural fit of those candidates whom you are considering for your target position.

As previously defined during construction of your high-performance model, measuring compatibility with the organization will require you to explore two primary areas:

1. The work environment itself.
2. The traits, characteristics, and behaviors of high performers in that environment.

To increase the probability of selecting high performers, we need to determine whether they will find the work environment motivating and stimulating. Next, we will need to compare these candidates to the profiles of existing high performers in the current work environment, to be sure that they will exhibit the behaviors that the organization historically has supported and rewarded.

The work you have already done in constructing the "organizational compatibility" portion of your predictive model in the previous chapter will provide you with some excellent measuring sticks against which to gauge prospective employment candidates. It makes sense, then, to utilize these standards in designing your interview approach for measuring and predicting fit with organizational culture.

Our approach here will be to systematically examine each component of the "cultural compatibility" section of the predictive model and then use these components to construct behaviorally based interview questions. We will start with the "work environment" section.

Work Environment

The work environment is what it is, and candidates either fit it or they don't. If they don't, they will be unhappy, demotivated, and generally unproductive. Conversely, if they fit the work environment rather well, they will be stimulated, motivated, happy, and generally quite productive. Picking high performers, therefore, requires that you become skilled at measuring just how well candidates will fit the work environment.

The preceding chapter recommended exploring eight "points of inquiry" to achieve a reasonable level of insight regarding the type of work environment which a given candidate will find stimulating and motivational. These are:

1. General work environment
2. Nature or type of work
3. Decision-making environment
4. Resource allocation process

5. Nature of working relationships (outside immediate work group)

6. Nature of working relationships (within immediate work group)

7. Opportunity for participation in business planning and strategy formulation

8. Management philosophy and style

Although there are certainly other possible areas of exploration, these eight factors are believed sufficient to provide a fairly comprehensive sampling of a given work environment and, for the purpose of interview design, should serve us quite well.

By exploring a candidate's preferences in each of these focal areas, we will acquire some excellent insight regarding the work environment that the candidate finds motivational and satisfying. Our job, then, is to compare what we have found out about the candidate's preferred work environment with the work environment we actually have to offer. This direct comparison will provide a reliable basis for determining whether there will be a good cultural fit and for predicting if the candidate will be both stimulated and productive by this environment.

Since we did not take much time in the preceding chapter to discuss work environment, some further information on this subject may be useful before proceeding with interview design for this important selection component.

Chapter 5 provided a process for development of your target job work environment profile, which you then incorporated into your high-performance, predictive model. Well, I am now going to show you how such a work environment profile can be used to evaluate prospective candidates and ascertain their compatibility with organizational culture.

To do this, I will first present a sample profile of a given work environment and then describe a hypothetical candidate profile. Comparing the two profiles (candidate vs. company) will show just how effective a tool this comparison technique can be when determining a candidate's fit with organizational culture.

SAMPLE ORGANIZATIONAL PROFILE

Actual Work Environment

General Work Environment

High pressure. Large volume of work. Tight deadlines. Plenty of homework. Some Saturday and Sunday work required.

Type of Work

Detailed, analytical work requiring high level of accuracy and good mathematical/statistical skills. Requires numerous repetitive calculations.

Decision-Making Environment

Little freedom to make independent decisions. All major decisions made at the top. Well-defined guidelines and procedures for most decisions at this job level.

Resource Allocation Process

Principal method for allocating resources is the budget process. Budgets set by top management with little input from this job level. Budget process rigid and inflexible. Exceptions difficult to obtain; require top management approval.

Basis for Effective Working Relationships (external functions)

Hard-nosed negotiations needed for effective relationships with other departments. Environment politically charged, with many turf issues. Disputes quickly elevated to higher level for resolution.

Basis for Effective Working Relationships (within function)

High pressure, fast-paced environment; little time for idle, social chitter-chatter. Intense, work-focused people with little inclination for establishing relationships on a personal level.

Role in Business Planning and Strategy Formulation

No role for position at this level. This activity performed at senior management level.

Management Philosophy and Style (within function)

Employees viewed as "operatives"—the "vessels through which work gets accomplished." Employees told what to do and how to do it; then expected to "get it done." Little provided in the way of personal or career development.

As you can see from this illustration, by following the guidelines in Chapter 5, a person can capture a usable organizational work environment profile for employee selection purposes. Now, let's look at a hypothetical candidate's "preferred work environment" profile, to see just how useful a selection tool the work environment profile can actually be.

SAMPLE CANDIDATE PROFILE

Preferred Work Environment

General Work Environment

Prefers structured but somewhat relaxed setting, where there is reasonable time to contemplate decisions. Some homework acceptable but values personal time and likes to keep business and personal time separate. Feels a good balance between the two is important.

Type of Work

Prefers work requiring strong mathematical, statistical, and computation skills. Likes new challenges and variety in work.

Decision-Making Environment

Likes an environment that provides broad overall guidelines and objectives, where there is the opportunity for independent decision making and judgment.

Resource Allocation Process

Prepared and submitted own budgets in all past positions. Believes this is important to ensure availability of adequate resources for getting the work done. Continuing involvement in budgeting and resource planning process described as "very important."

Basis for Effective Working Relationships (external functions)

Enjoys a collegial setting with mutual respect between functional areas important. Works best in an environment with "shared goals and an overall sense of teamwork." Believes the "overall mission of the business is more important than the raw political needs of a single group."

Basis for Effective Working Relationships (within function)

Prefers a "teamwork setting," where there is a "sense of shared goals and commitment to results." Works best in a "harmonious environment where there is a strong sense of interdependence and sharing." Enjoys the "social aspects of close working relationships."

Role in Planning and Strategy Formulation

Limited participation in overall business planning and formulation in previous positions. Although enjoys this participation, does not appear to be a critical factor in job satisfaction.

Management Philosophy and Style

Most motivated and productive when working in a heavily "participative" environment. Dislikes working in an environment "where boss makes all the decisions and there is no opportunity to contribute ideas."

Note: Quotation marks to represent actual statements made by the candidate during the interview discussion.

Okay, so you're going to accuse me of stacking the deck a bit! Well, I'm afraid that I'm going to have to plead guilty, as charged. But, the contrast does make a real point, doesn't it? Comparing this candidate's preferred work environment with the organization's actual work environment makes it obvious that this candidate is not going to blend well with the culture of the hiring organization. To the contrary, this lack of fit will all but guarantee intense employee dissatisfaction, unhappiness, low motivation, and substandard productivity.

Work environment, therefore, is a critical selection factor when choosing high performers. Where there is a poor match, we should reject the candidate and immediately move on in search of someone who will enjoy the type of work we have to offer and the environment in which that work will be performed.

Let's now return to the main topic of this chapter— interview design. If measuring candidate fit with the work environment is important to the selection of high performers, as we now know it is, what can we do from an interview design standpoint to guarantee that we select employees who will really fit in?

Again, we return to the concept of behaviorally based interviewing. Specifically, the type of work and work environment that elicited a high level of candidate motivation and satisfaction in the past will give us some good clues concerning the type of work environment that will maximize the same candidate's future motivation and satisfaction. Our interview strategy for measuring organizational compatibility, therefore, must focus on the candidate's past work environments to uncover the keys to his or her satisfaction and productivity. Here is a case where the "comparison/contrast" interview technique (see Chapter 3), can be unusually powerful.

You may wish to incorporate the following interview questions into your interview design. (Chapter 7 also contains some excellent questions on work environment.) These will prove particularly effective in measuring and predicting the probability of a fit with your organization's work environment. As with the preceding example, comparing your predictive model (as previously defined in your high-performance model; see Figure 5.7) and a candidate's preferred work environment should provide you with an excellent basis for making this important determination, and further ensuring the employment of high performers.

KEY INTERVIEW QUESTIONS

Work Environment

General Work Environment

1. In which of your previous positions did you feel most motivated and productive?

   What factors most influenced these positive feelings?

2. In which of your past positions did you feel least motivated and productive?

   Why? What key factors contributed to your feelings?

Type of Work

1. As you think about past jobs from a work content standpoint, which was most challenging and satisfying?

   Why? What was there about this type of work that you found satisfying?

2. Again, as you view your past positions from a work content standpoint, which did you find least satisfying and why?

   What specific factors most contributed to this lesser satisfaction?

3. How would you describe the type of work you most like to do?

   From a work content standpoint, what factors are most important to you?

Decision Making, Resource Allocation, Business Planning, and Strategy Formulation

Given a choice between the following two work environments, in which of these would you feel most motivated and productive. Why? Cite some examples from your past work history.

   a. A work environment that requires broad involvement in decision making, provides for heavy involvement in determination of budgets and planning resource allocation, and where you are only answerable to senior management for your results.

b. A work environment that focuses heavily on "operations" (getting things done) with little or no need to get involved with the details of budgeting, resource planning and allocation, or business planning and strategy—an environment where you are held closely accountable to management for daily results.

Effective Working Relationships (external functions)

1. As you think about your working relationships with other departments and functions, in which of your past positions did you find these external relationships particularly satisfying? What factors most influenced your positive feelings?

2. By contrast, in which of your past positions did you feel that your relationships with others outside your department were least productive and satisfying? What key factors influenced your feelings?

Effective Working Relationships (within function)

1. In which of your previous positions did you most enjoy working with your immediate work group? What key factors made this relationship particularly enjoyable?

2. In which of your past positions did you find working relationships within your immediate work group least rewarding? What major factors fostered these feelings?

Management Philosophy and Style

1. For which of your past bosses did you most enjoy working?
   a. What about this working relationship made it so satisfying?
   b. What about this boss's management style did you find particularly pleasing?
   c. How did you respond to this style, and why?

2. Of your past bosses, for whom did you least enjoy working?
   a. What was there about this boss's management style that caused you to feel this way?

b. What specific traits and characteristics of this boss did you find most displeasing?

c. How did this affect you, and why?

Profile of High Performers

A second component of cultural fit, as you may recall from the preceding chapter, is the profile of the organization's current or past high performers who have held the position in question. Understanding what is unique or different about this group gives us strong clues about what traits, characteristics, and behaviors are required for high performance in the firm's work environment.

The final step in completing your interview design, as you might suspect, therefore is to design a good set of interview questions for effectively probing the personal profiles of prospective employment candidates. These candidate profiles are then compared with the profiles of successful employees. Since you already identified the traits, characteristics, and behaviors of high performers as part of your high-performance, predictive model (see Chapter 5), it is now a matter of using the interview to construct an accurate profile of candidates that will enable the comparison with the high-performance model.

The basic areas that need to be probed to construct this candidate profile are:

1. Key traits, characteristics, and behaviors.
2. Preferred business philosophy/style (if a manager).
3. Preferred operating style.
4. Preferred personal style.

To be effective, therefore, the interview design must incorporate questions to get behaviorally based information that accurately describes prospective candidates in each of these four focal areas. The resultant composite candidate profile should provide us with an excellent basis for comparison with our high-performance model and for predicting the probability of selecting someone who will be productive and successful in our work culture.

Essentially, construction of a candidate profile for our purposes here focuses on designing interview questions that target:

1. Peer observations.
2. Observations of past bosses.
3. Subordinate observations (if a manager).
4. Self-observations.

As the interviewer, you need to look for distinct patterns that emerge concerning the candidate traits, characteristics, and behaviors in these areas during the interview discussion. Since, at this point in the interview and selection process, you must rely on the candidate's impression of how others would describe him or her, it is particularly important to pay attention to the general, repetitive themes that emerge from the answers to your questions. Fortunately, before an offer is made, you will usually have the benefit of reference check discussions to verify the accuracy of the information supplied by the candidate during this phase of the interview process.

Rather than be redundant, I would like to direct your attention to the "personal profile" section of the interview plan (Figure 6.2), where I have included a set of well-constructed interview questions to thoroughly probe this important selection factor. (A more extensive list of interview questions designed to probe a candidate's "personal profile" appears in Chapter 7; see the headings "Traits and Characteristics,"

"Business Philosophy," and "Operating Style.") If you prefer, you can construct your own questions for this section of the interview plan, using the sample questions as a guide.

At this point, you have all the ammunition you need to prepare a comprehensive, thorough interview plan covering all three of the factors critical to the selection of high performers—job fit, strategic fit, and cultural fit. Effective interviewing requires both time and effort, but the payoff of consistently selecting high-performing personnel is well worth the time and effort. It can well mean the difference between financial failure and competitive superiority in the marketplace. Much of your firm's success hinges squarely on the effectiveness of your employee selection process.

I. MEASURING JOB AND PROJECT KNOWLEDGE

  A. FUNCTIONAL ACCOUNTABILITY

    1. Key Problem 1

    _____

    _____

    _____

    2. Key Problem 2

    _____

    _____

    _____

    3. Key Problem 3

    _____

    _____

    _____

    4. Key Problem 4

    _____

    _____

    _____

    5. Key Problem 5

    _____

    _____

    _____

    6. Key Problem 6

    _____

    _____

    _____

    7. Key Problem 7

    _____

    _____

    _____

    8. Key Problem 8

    _____

    _____

    _____

    9. Key Problem 9

    _____

    _____

    _____

Figure 6.2 *Interview Plan*

10. Key Problem 10

_____
_____
_____

B. PROJECT ACCOUNTABILITIES
   1. Key Problem 1

_____
_____
_____

   2. Key Problem 2

_____
_____
_____

   3. Key Problem 3

_____
_____
_____

   4. Key Problem 4

_____
_____
_____

   5. Key Problem 5

_____
_____
_____

   6. Key Problem 6

_____
_____
_____

II. MEASURING STRATEGIC KNOWLEDGE
   A. KEY PROBLEM/BARRIER 1

_____
_____
_____

   B. KEY PROBLEM/BARRIER 2

_____
_____
_____

Figure 6.2   *(continued)*

C. KEY PROBLEM/BARRIER 3

_____
_____
_____
_____

D. KEY PROBLEM/BARRIER 4

_____
_____
_____
_____

E. KEY PROBLEM/BARRIER 5

_____
_____
_____
_____

F. KEY PROBLEM/BARRIER 6

_____
_____
_____
_____

III. MEASURING MOTIVATION TO SOLVE KEY PROBLEMS

  A. KEY INTERVIEW QUESTIONS

1. From a technical challenge standpoint (the kinds of problems you were faced with), which of your past jobs was most stimulating?

2. What was there about these problems that you found interesting?

3. Of your past positions, from a technical challenge standpoint, which did you find least stimulating?

4. What was there about the problems you had to face that made this position less satisfying?

5. What kinds of problems do you most enjoy tackling? Why?

   a. Give me some examples of such problems you faced.

   b. What did you enjoy about them?

6. What types of problems do you least enjoy tacking? Why?

   a. Give me some examples of such problems you faced.

   b. What was there about them that you least enjoyed?

Figure 6.2   *(continued)*

IV. MEASURING FIT WITH ORGANIZATIONAL CULTURE

(*Note:* See Chapter 7 for additional sample questions.)

A. WORK ENVIRONMENT

1. *General Work Environment*
   a. In which of your past positions did you feel most motivated and productive?
   b. What factors most influenced these feelings?
   c. In which of your past positions did you feel least motivated and productive?
   d. What factors most contributed to your feelings?

2. *Type of Work*
   a. From a work content standpoint, which of your past positions was most challenging and rewarding?
   b. What was there about this work that you found so stimulating?
   c. From a work content viewpoint, which of your previous positions was least satisfying?
   d. What was there about this work that you found less satisfying?
   e. From a work content standpoint, what type of work do you most like to do?

3. *Decision Making, Resource Allocation, Business Planning, Strategy Formulation*

   Given a choice between the following two work environments, which would you most enjoy? Why?
   a. (Using the preceding categories, describe the opposite of your work environment.)

   _____
   _____
   _____
   _____
   _____
   _____
   _____
   _____
   _____

Figure 6.2 *(continued)*

b. (Using the preceding categories, describe your actual work environment.)

_____
_____
_____
_____
_____
_____
_____
_____
_____

4. *Effective Working Relationships* (outside immediate work group)

   a. As you think of working relationships with other functions (outside your own department), in which of your previous positions were you most effective?

   b. What factors most influenced your effectiveness?

   c. In which of your past positions did you have the most effective working relationship with fellow department members?

   d. What factors contributed to this effective relationship?

5. *Management Philosophy and Style*

   a. For which of your past bosses did you most enjoy working?

   b. What traits did this boss exhibit that you found particularly pleasing?

   c. How did you respond to these traits? Why?

   d. For which of your past bosses did you least enjoy working?

   e. What traits did this boss exhibit that you found less pleasing?

   f. How did you respond to these traits? Why?

B. PERSONAL PROFILE

1. If we had two or three persons (with whom you work closely) in the room with us and asked them to describe you, what three or four things would they likely say about you rather quickly?

2. In what ways would they describe you as being particularly effective?

Figure 6.2   *(continued)*

3. What two or three areas would they quickly identify as areas for improvement, to increase your overall effectiveness?

4. During past performance evaluations, what traits and characteristics have been frequently used to categorize you in the following areas:

    a. Your work or operating style?

    b. Your personal style?

    c. Notable traits, characteristics, and behaviors?

    d. Areas in which you are particularly strong?

    e. Areas for development and improvement?

    f. Your management style (if a manager)?

5. If we were to ask two or three of your subordinates to describe your management style, what would they likely say?

    a. What areas would they select as areas of management strength? Why?

    b. What two or three areas would they likely cite for improvement? Why?

6. Describe your overall business philosophy.

    a. What is important to overall business success?

    b. Why are these things important?

7. What five or six adjectives do you feel best describe you as others see you?

8. If you could change one thing about yourself, to add to your effectiveness, what would it be?

    a. How would you change?

    b. Why?

Figure 6.2   *(continued)*

Interview Designer's Guide: 500+ Great Questions

This chapter is a companion to the preceding chapter on interview design. It contains over 500 well-constructed, behaviorally based interview questions covering some 32 topical areas. I strongly recommend that you use the questions in this chapter in developing your interview plan (see Figure 6.2).

The majority of the interview questions in this chapter are based on sound behavioral interview techniques and will help you collect solid behavioral evidence of a candidate's qualifications, traits, characteristics, and behavioral tendencies. The answers to these questions, when incorporated into your interview design and used in conjunction with your predictive model, should substantially improve your ability to identify and hire high performers.

The following Topic Index will facilitate use of the information in this chapter. By selecting a given subject area (which is important to effective candidate job performance of your target position), you will find an array of interview questions that will prove extremely effective in helping you evaluate a candidate's qualifications against your predictive model. These questions can then be incorporated into your interview plan at the end of Chapter 6.

TOPIC INDEX

Strengths

1. What key factors have accounted for your career success to date?

2. What do you consider to be some of your most outstanding qualities?

3. What is your greatest strength or asset?

4. In what areas have others been particularly complimentary about your abilities? Why?

5. During past performance reviews, what have been consistently cited as your major assets? Why?

6. From a performance standpoint, what do you consider your major attributes?

7. If I were to check your references with two or three of your co-workers, in what areas would they describe you as particularly effective?

8. In viewing your candidacy for this position, in what areas do you feel you would be a particularly strong performer? Why?

9. Describe your three greatest strengths and tell me how you used them to bring about improvements in your job.

10. What two or three major accomplishments best demonstrate your key strengths?

11. In what ways are your qualifications unique or distinctive?

12. What do your co-workers most admire about you? Why?

13. What would your current boss describe as your three greatest assets? Why?

14. When compared with other members of your department, where do you most excel?

15. In what areas can others totally rely on your ability?

16. What would a thorough reference check reveal as your strongest attributes?

17. During the past two years, in what aspect of your work have you most excelled?

18. On a scale of 1 to 10 (1 being "nonexistent," 10 being "without peer"), which of your qualifications would you rate at the 9 and 10 level?

19. If you had to cite a single skill or attribute that has most contributed to your career success, what would it be? Why?

20. Describe how your major accomplishments demonstrate your ability to effectively use some of your key strengths and capabilities.

Weaknesses

1. What has been your single biggest work-related failure to date? Why?

2. From a work standpoint, what has been your biggest shortcoming? Why?

3. Each of us have areas where we could improve performance. In what areas could you improve your overall performance?

4. What areas have been suggested to you for improvement by your current boss?

5. As you view your overall qualifications for this position, what do you see as some of your development needs?

6. What aspect of your overall capabilities would you most like to improve?

7. What steps have you taken in the past year to improve your overall performance? Why?

8. From an overall effectiveness standpoint, what would you most like to improve that would enhance your value to your employer?

9. During a thorough reference check, what areas can we expect to find where your overall performance and effectiveness might be improved?

10. During past performance reviews, what are some of the areas that have been identified for improvement?

11. In what ways could you improve your overall job performance?

12. In what ways could you improve your effectiveness with others?

13. What would you cite as the three areas of your performance that could most be improved?

14. What aspects of your current position could be better performed, and what kind of improvement could be made?

15. If we asked two or three of your peers who know you well, to be somewhat critical of your performance, what two or three improvement areas would they likely identify? Why?

16. If you could, what two things would you most like to change about yourself to improve your overall effectiveness—and why?

17. What are you currently doing to improve your overall performance?

18. In what ways could you improve your interpersonal skills and effectiveness?

19. In what ways could you enhance your overall professional capability?

20. What aspect of your overall qualifications has most stood in the way of your career advancement to date?

Job Performance

1. Tell me about your recent salary increases—how well did they reflect your performance and contributions?

2. In what ways has your job changed since you first entered the function?

3. What do you consider your two or three most significant accomplishments?

   a. In your current position?

   b. Since joining your current company?

   c. In your career?

4. In checking your references, what would your boss tell me about your performance?

   a. What aspects of the job would he or she say you perform well?

   b. What areas would he or she indicate could be improved?

5. If I talked with two or three of your peers who work closely with you and are most familiar with your work, what would they cite as:

   a. Your biggest contributions to the department or function?

   b. One or two areas where you could improve your overall performance?

6. What have been your last 3 performance evaluation ratings? Why?

7. In what areas does your performance excel?

8. In what areas could your overall performance be most improved?

9. Of which job accomplishments are you most proud? Why?

10. Of which performance factors are you least proud? Why?

11. What were your key job objectives during this past year, and how well did you perform against each?

12. What evidence can you cite to support your overall effectiveness during this past year?

13. With what aspects of your current performance are you least satisfied?

   a. What kind of improvement could be realized?

   b. What are you doing to improve in these areas?

14. What key accomplishments can you cite that suggest you are an excellent candidate for this position?

15. Of which of your accomplishments are you most proud? Why?

16. If we asked your fellow workers to rate your overall performance on a scale of 1 to 10 (1 low, 5 average, 10 outstanding), where do you feel they would rate you? Why?

   a. What factors would they rate high? Why?

   b. What factors would they rate low? Why?

17. Based on how you feel your boss would rate your current job performance, what areas would he or she cite as:

   a. Exceeding expectations? Why?

   b. Meeting expectations?

   c. Falling short of expectations? Why?

18. What key accomplishments best exemplify your overall qualifications for this job?

19. How does your performance compare with that of others in your department?

    a. Where do you excel?

    b. Where could you improve?

20. As you review your overall performance during the past year:

    a. Of which accomplishments are you most proud?

    b. Of which of your accomplishments are you least proud? Why?

    c. How would you categorize the quantity of your work? Why?

    d. How would you categorize the quality of your work? Why?

Interpersonal Skills

1. With what kind of people do you most enjoy working? Why?

2. With what kind of people do you have difficulty working? Why?

3. Describe your relationship with your past boss.

    a. In what areas did you agree?

    b. In what areas did you disagree? Why?

    c. What did you do to resolve your differences?

4. With which of your past work groups did you most enjoy working?

5. What factors most influenced your positive feelings?

6. With which of your past work groups did you least enjoy working?

    a. What accounted for your lack of enjoyment?

    b. What did you do about it?

    c. What was the outcome?

7. How would you describe your relationships with others outside your immediate department? Why?

8. Tell me about a time when you had a major conflict with another employee.

    a. What was the cause of the conflict?

    b. What things did you do to alleviate the problem?

    c. What were the results?

9. In which of your past positions did you feel most comfortable (had a sense of belonging or fitting in the group)?

10. In which of your past positions did you feel least comfortable (had a sense of not belonging or fitting in the group)?

    a. What contributed to your uneasiness?

    b. What did you do to ease these feelings?

11. If, during a reference check, I asked your boss to describe your interpersonal skills, what would he or she likely tell me about your overall effectiveness with others?

    a. What aspects of your interpersonal skills would he or she rate as particularly effective?

    b. What aspects of your interpersonal effectiveness would he or she cite as needing improvement? Why?

12. What aspects of your interpersonal skills would you most like to improve? Why?

13. When confronted by someone who is particularly angry with you, what do you do?

14. If someone is continuously critical of you and appears not to like you, what do you do?

15. If you sense you are not fitting in well with a group and feel that you are being treated as an outsider, what would you do?

16. What examples can you cite that best demonstrate your ability to relate well to others?

17. In which of your past positions did you feel most isolated and alone?

    a. What caused you to feel this way?

    b. What did you do about it?

18. What could you do that would most improve your effectiveness with others?

19. Which of your skills would you rate higher?

    a. Your "technical" skills?

    b. Your "interpersonal" skills?

    c. Why?

20. Do you feel it is more important to be:

    a. Well liked by others?

    b. Admired for being effective?

    c. Why?

Preferred Type of Work

1. From a job content standpoint, which of your past positions did you enjoy most? Why?

2. From a job content standpoint, which of your past positions did you least enjoy? Why?

3. What type of work do you find most stimulating and rewarding? Why?

4. What type of work do you find least stimulating and rewarding? Why?

5. Which of your past positions provided the most interesting challenges?

   a. What were these challenges?

   b. What made them interesting?

6. Which of your past positions did you find least challenging?

   a. Why did you find it unchallenging?

   b. What factors influenced your feelings?

7. How would you describe the type of work you most like to do?

8. How would you categorize the kind of work you least like doing?

9. How would you compare the type of work you did at the Wallace Company with the work you did at Dana Corporation?

   a. Which work did you like most? Why?

   b. Which work did you like least? Why?

10. In which of your past positions were you most motivated and productive?

    a. What work factors accounted for this motivation?

    b. What factors most affected your positive feelings?

    c. The absence of what factors enhanced your positive outlook?

11. What type of work do you find most satisfying from a professional standpoint?

12. What type of work do you find least satisfying from a professional standpoint?

13. What have you learned from your past work experience about the type of work you most enjoy doing?

14. What has your experience taught you about the type of work you least enjoy doing?

15. What aspects of your position as engineer at Fullerton Company did you find particularly enjoyable? Why?

16. What aspects of your engineering position at Fullerton Company did you find least satisfying? Why?

17. With what aspects of your job at General Electric were you most comfortable? Why?

18. With what aspects of your job at General Electric were you least comfortable? Why?

19. From a job content standpoint, what factors most influence your level of job satisfaction?

    a. What factors enhance job satisfaction?

    b. What factors detract from job satisfaction?

20. How would you describe the "ideal job" from a work content standpoint?

Preferred Work Environment

1. In which of your past work environments were you happiest?

    a. Why were you happy?

    b. What specific factors contributed to your feelings?

2. In which of your past work environments were you least happy?

    a. Why were you unhappy?

    b. What factors most caused your unhappiness?

3. Compare the work environment at Bostwich Corporation with that of Wharton Company.

   a. Which environment was more satisfying? Why?

   b. Which environment was less satisfying? Why?

4. What did you like most about the work environment at Blair Industries?

5. What did you like least about the work environment at Blair?

6. What aspects of the work environment at Johnson & Johnson did you find most stimulating? Why?

7. What aspects of the work environment at Johnson & Johnson did you find least stimulating? What accounted for this lack of stimulation?

8. In which of your past work environments did you feel you had greatest influence and impact? Why?

9. In which of your past work environments did you feel you had the least amount of influence and impact? What caused these feelings?

10. What type of work environment do you find motivational and stimulating?

11. What type of work environment do you find demotivating? Why?

12. How could your current work environment be made more interesting and exciting.

    a. What things would you change?

    b. In what ways would you change them?

13. On a scale of 1 to 10 (1 low, 10 high) where would you rate your level of satisfaction with your current work environment?

    a. What factors would you rate high? Why?

    b. What factors would you rate low? Why?

14. In what kind of work environment are you most productive?

15. In what kind of work environment are you least productive?

16. What four or five things are important to you in a work environment?

    a. Which is the most important? Why?

    b. Which is the least important? Why?

17. How would you describe the "ideal work environment"?

    a. What things would be present? Why?

    b. What things would be absent? Why?

18. Which of your past work environments came closest to your "ideal"?

    a. What factors did you find particularly appealing?

    b. How would you rank their importance, and why?

19. Describe the work environment in which you were most productive.

    a. What accounted for your effectiveness?

    b. Which factors were most influential?

20. How would you describe your current work environment?

    a. What do you find particularly satisfying?

    b. What improvements would you like to see? Why?

Traits and Characteristics

(*Note:* All of these questions are to be asked only in the context of job and work effectiveness—not impact on personal life.)

1. How would you describe yourself?

2. What five or six adjectives best describe you?

3. If we had three or four of your close associates with us and asked them to describe you, what would they likely say?

4. If we asked your current manager to list three or four of your positive traits and characteristics, what would he or she say?

5. If we asked the same manager to describe those traits and characteristics he or she finds less pleasing, what would he or she say?

6. What words best describe your personal style?

7. Which of your personal traits and characteristics have been most helpful in your career?

8. Which of your personal traits and characteristics do you feel have most hindered your career progress?

9. In past performance reviews, which of your personal traits and characteristics have often been cited as strengths?

10. In past performance evaluations, which of your personal traits and characteristics have been cited as areas for improvement?

11. In your most intimate conversations with family and/or close friends, what have people said they most like about you?

12. In similar confidential conversations, what aspects of your personal style have been suggested as areas for improvement?

13. Which of your traits and characteristics do you find most frustrating?

14. Of which of your personal traits and characteristics are you most proud, and why?

15. Of which of your personal traits and characteristics are you least proud? Why?

16. What is there about yourself that you would most like to change?

    a. How would you change?

    b. Why?

17. Which of your personal traits and characteristics most enhance your effectiveness in dealing with others?

18. Which of your traits and characteristics sometimes get in the way of your relationships with others?

19. What of your personal traits and characteristics best suit you for this particular job?

20. To what aspects of your personal style are you most sensitive and try continuously to improve?

Business Philosophy

1. How would you describe your overall business philosophy?

2. Give me three examples of things you do in your daily operations that reflect your business beliefs.

3. What do you feel is essential to having a successful business environment?

4. What do you feel are sound principles for operating a successful business?

5. What values are important to sustain a successful business in the long run?

6. If you were to structure a set of basic values and beliefs on which to build a successful business enterprise, what would you include?

7. What kinds of values and beliefs do you feel are detrimental to operation of a successful business enterprise?

8. Why, in your judgment, are certain businesses successful?

9. In your judgment, what factors account for most business failures?

10. If you could structure the ideal business environment, what kinds of behaviors would you encourage and reward? Why?

11. What kinds of behaviors would you discourage and even punish? Why?

12. What do you believe are universal characteristics of successful organizations?

    a. What do such organizations stand for?

    b. What are their guiding principles?

13. What do you believe are universal characteristics of organizations that fail?

    a. What do such organizations stand for?

    b. By what kind of principles do they operate?

    c. What key principles are they missing?

14. Demonstrate how some of your key accomplishments reflect your basic principles and beliefs about what is needed for successful business performance.

15. How do successful business organizations manage their employees?

16. Contrast this with unsuccessful businesses.

17. How do successful organizations plan and allocate their resources?

18. Contrast this with less successful organizations.

19. Describe the planning and decision-making processes important to successful business operations.

20. In your opinion, what do unsuccessful organizations' planning and decision-making processes look like? What are they missing?

21. What kinds of behaviors do highly successful companies reward? Why?

22. What kinds of behaviors do less successful companies reward? Why?

Operating Style

1. How would you categorize your operating style—the way you go about doing your work?

2. How would you compare your operating style with others in your function?

3. In what way is it unique or distinctive?

4. What benefits do you feel are derived by operating in this manner?

5. What kind of operating style do you feel is important to good performance? Why?

6. What kind of operating style do you feel is not conducive to good performance? Why?

7. What basic values and beliefs do you feel are important to good performance?

8. What do you believe about the basic values and beliefs of poor performers?

9. What do they have in common?

10. Contrast the values and beliefs of good performers with those of poor performers.

    a. In what ways are they different?

    b. What distinguishes good performers?

    c. What distinguishes poor performers?

11. What are the basic work principles by which you try to operate?

12. Why are these important to you?

13. How are these basic work principles reflected in your work and job accomplishments?

14. Give me some recent examples of how these work or operating principles benefited your performance.

    a. What principles did you employ?

    b. How did you behave?

    c. What was the result?

15. Give me an example of where you abandoned one of your basic work principles, and it backfired on you.

    a. What was the circumstance?

    b. What principle did you abandon?

    c. Why did you abandon this principle?

    d. What was the result?

    e. What did you learn from this experience?

16. What do you believe are the key operating or work principles by which most successful people operate? Why?

17. What key operating or work principles, in your judgment, are most frequently ignored by poor performers?

18. If I asked others in your work group, based on their observation of your work style, to describe what they believe is your operating philosophy—what would they likely say?

19. How is your operating philosophy reflected in the way you do your work?

20. If, during a reference check, I asked your past bosses to categorize your work style, what description would they most likely agree on?

Management Style, Philosophy, and Effectiveness

1. What do you believe are the characteristics of an effective manager?

   a. What are the key attributes?

   b. Which are most important, and why?

2. How would you describe your management philosophy?

3. How would you describe your overall management process—the process you use to manage others?

4. With which of the following management styles are you most comfortable?

   a. *Controlling.* Like to make most decisions personally and give close direction to others.

   b. *Participative.* Like to involve others in the decision-making process as much as possible, and see my principal roles as facilitator, teacher, coach.

5. If we asked your immediate subordinates to describe your management style, what would they likely say?

   a. In what areas would they be complimentary?

   b. What areas would they cite for improvement?

6. In past performance reviews, what kinds of things have been said about your effectiveness as a manager?

   a. What have been key managerial strengths?

   b. What areas have been suggested for improvement? Why?

7. What aspects of your management style have made you particularly effective in the management and motivation of others?

8. In what areas could you most improve your overall effectiveness as a manager of others?

9. What do you believe is the proper role of a manager? Why?

10. What do you see as the key difference between a leader and a manager?

11. Are you more a manager or a leader? Why?

12. Describe your overall planning process.

13. What are some of the techniques you use to motivate poor performers?

    a. Give me some examples of how you have used these techniques.

    b. What results did you get?

    c. How could these have been improved?

14. What is the toughest decision you have had to make as a manager?

    a. Why was it tough?

    b. What did you decide?

    c. What were the results?

15. How do you go about evaluating individual employee performance?

    a. What is your basis for evaluation?

    b. What standards do you use?

    c. How do you measure against these standards?

16. Describe your process for monitoring and controlling overall department operations and performance.

    a. What are the performance benchmarks?

    b. What are your monitoring techniques?

    c. What controls do you exercise?

17. Describe your approach to employee development.

    a. How do you determine development needs?

    b. How are these communicated?

    c. How is accountability assigned?

    d. What successes have you had?

    e. How could you be more effective in this area?

18. Describe your process for employee selection.

    a. How do you go about defining the candidate specification?

    b. Describe your interview process.

    c. What evidence can you provide of your effectiveness in the selection of others?

    d. How could you improve this process?

19. What tangible, measurable evidence can you cite for your effectiveness as a manager?

20. In what ways could you most improve your overall managerial effectiveness?

Education

1. How did your education prepare you for your career?

2. What do you most value about your education? Why?

3. How has your education helped you with your current job?

4. In what ways has your education helped you to be more productive?

5. How appropriate do you feel your education has been in preparing you for your profession?

6. What could you do educationally to improve your overall effectiveness in your work?

7. What specific courses have been most helpful to you in performing your job? How have you used them?

8. How did you come to select Bucknell University; what key factors most influenced your decision?

9. What led to your decision to major in accounting?

10. In what courses did you do best? Why?

11. What were your worst courses? Why?

12. What were the key benefits of attending Bucknell?

13. In what ways have you benefited from your decision to be an accounting major?

14. What did you like most about your educational experience?

15. What did you least like about your educational experience?

16. If you could repeat your educational experience, what would you do differently? Why?

17. What professor most influenced your life? How?

18. What was there about being an engineering major that you found most appealing?

19. How have you used your education to your benefit?

20. What aspect of your life has your education most affected?

Preferred Boss's Style

1. Who was the best boss you ever had?

2. What were some of this boss's key traits and characteristics?

3. What effect did these have on you? Why?

4. Describe your current boss.

   a. What do you most like about him or her? Why?

   b. What do you like least about him or her? Why?

5. How would you describe your relationship with your current boss?

   a. In what areas do you agree?

   b. In what areas do you disagree? Why?

6. If there were something that you could improve about your current boss:

   a. What would it be?

   b. What change would you make?

   c. Why?

7. What about your boss's management approach do you find motivational? Why?

8. What about your boss's management approach do you find frustrating and particularly demotivating? Why?

9. How would you categorize the "ideal" boss?

   a. What would be his or her management philosophy?

   b. What would be his or her management style?

   c. In what ways would you find this philosophy and style beneficial to you?

   d. Why would you find this person stimulating to work for?

10. How would you categorize the "worst" boss?

   a. What would be his or her management philosophy?

   b. What would be his or her management style?

    c. In what ways would you find this philosophy and style detrimental to you?

    d. Why would you find this person demotivating?

11. How would you categorize the traits and attributes of a good manager? Why are these important?

12. How would you categorize the traits and attributes of a poor manager?

13. What type of manager do you find inspirational and motivational? Why?

14. What type of manager do you find uninspiring and demotivating? Why?

15. Describe your relationship with your past boss.

16. What did you like most about this boss? Why?

17. What did you like least about this boss? Why?

18. What is characteristic of some of the best bosses you have had? What did they have in common?

19. What is characteristic about some of the worst bosses you have had? What did they have in common?

20. Which of your past bosses would you most like to emulate? Why?

Early Background (Childhood)

1. Describe the environment in which you grew up.

2. What are some of the basic values you learned early on, that you still hold as important today?

3. What do you remember about your life as a child?

    a. What did you most value?

    b. What did you least value?

4. Who most influenced you as a child?

   a. In what ways did they influence you?

   b. What did you learn from this relationship?

   c. In what ways has this been beneficial?

5. What were the high points of your childhood? Why are these important to you?

6. What did you most like about being a child?

7. What did you least like about being a child?

8. What were some of your most meaningful childhood accomplishments and why were these important?

9. Describe your relationship with your brothers and/or sisters (if any).

10. With whom did you most get along? Why?

11. With whom did you least get along? Why?

12. What beliefs do you hold deeply as a result of your early life experiences?

13. What key principles do you now live by that were formulated during your childhood? Why are these important to you?

14. How would you categorize your role in the family?

15. For what kind of things were you recognized and rewarded by your family?

16. What kind of activity and behavior was discouraged and/or punished by your parents?

17. How would you describe your relationship with your parents?

   a. With your father?

   b. With your mother?

18. In what ways did your father most influence your life?

19. In what ways did your mother most influence your life?

20. What was your most valuable childhood experience? Why was this significant?

MISCELLANEOUS AREAS

Creativity

1. What are the various approaches that could be used to address the following problem [describe problem]?

   a. Cite as many approaches as you can.

   b. Demonstrate what you believe to be a creative approach that will optimize results.

2. Give me an example of something very creative that you did.

   a. Why was it creative?

   b. What were the alternative approaches you considered?

   c. Why was this a particularly creative solution?

Willingness to Take Risks

1. What was the biggest business risk you have ever taken?

   a. Why was it risky?

   b. What prompted you to take the risk?

   c. What was the outcome?

2. In hindsight, when during your business life do you most regret not having taken a particular risk?

   a. What was the nature of the risk?

   b. Why didn't you pursue this risk?

3. What factors most influence your willingness to take a risk?

Analytical Ability

1. What is, perhaps, the most complex business analysis you have had to make?

    a. What factors made it complex?

    b. How did you tackle this task?

    c. How did your result reflect the effectiveness of your analytical abilities?

2. Describe how you would approach the following complex problem [describe problem].

    a. What approach would you take?

    b. Why would you choose this method?

Judgment

1. What examples can you cite of your ability to apply prudent judgment in a delicate situation?

    a. Why was the situation delicate?

    b. What did you do?

    c. Why did you do it?

    d. What was the outcome?

2. Faced with the decision to hire an exceptionally well-qualified candidate or the boss's daughter (who is only marginally qualified for the position), what would you do?

    a. Why would you make this decision?

    b. How would you manage the obvious sensitivities?

Persistence

1. Describe a work situation where you faced incredible odds but prevailed.

    a. What were the odds you faced?

    b. Why was there so much resistance?

    c. Why did you prevail?

2. Describe a work situation where you knew you were right, but the odds of winning were such that you felt you had to abandon your position.

    a. What odds did you face?

    b. How great was the resistance?

    c. What approaches did you use?

    d. How long did you fight?

    e. What factors persuaded you to abandon your position?

Planning and Organizational Skills

1. Describe your planning process.

    a. How often do you do planning?

    b. What are the steps in your planning process?

    c. How important is planning to organizational success?

    d. When can planning get in the way of results?

2. How do you go about organizing your work?

    a. What is your basis for organizing?

    b. How do you establish priorities?

    c. What impact has organization had on your results?

Communications Skills

1. Give me an example of a complex communications problem that you faced.

   a. What made it complex?

   b. Why was it difficult to communicate?

   c. How did you solve this problem? Why?

   d. How effective were the communications?

   e. What evidence do you have of this effectiveness?

   f. How might you have further improved the communications?

2. Are you more skilled at verbal or written communication? Why?

Integrity

1. Give me an example of a situation that required you to compromise one of your basic principles.

   a. What was the situation?

   b. What principle did you compromise?

   c. Why did you compromise?

   d. How did you feel about it?

2. If you caught one of your most valued employees doing something dishonest, what would you do?

Assertiveness

1. If your boss told you that you had a "stupid idea," but you knew it was a very good one, what would you do?

2. Someone in another department, with whom you have infrequent contact, has been saying some uncomplimentary things about you; what would you do?

Openness

1. What do you feel is your greatest shortcoming as far as your ability to perform this position?

2. What was the dumbest business decision you ever made?

Self-Assessment (for Target Position)

1. If you were the employer, knowing what you know about your overall qualifications for this position, what would be your greatest concern? Why?

2. With what aspects of this position are you most comfortable?

3. With what aspects of this position are you least comfortable? Why?

Drive and Motivation

1. Give me some examples of things you have done that go considerably beyond what is required by your job.

2. What basis do you use for measuring your own performance?

3. What aspects of your job performance are you least satisfied with, and what are you doing about it?

4. What things are you currently doing to improve your overall performance and results?

Ambition

1. What goals have you set for yourself in life?

2. By what standards do you measure your personal success?

3. What plans do you have for self-improvement and personal development?

4. What are your career expectations:

   a. Over the next three to five years?

   b. Ultimately?

Flexibility and Adaptability

1. During your career, what was the most difficult adjustment you have had to make?

   a. What was the situation?

   b. Why was this a difficult adjustment?

   c. What did you do?

   d. What happened as a result of your actions?

2. If you had an altercation with your boss and were told that you were being "rigid and inflexible" in your view, what would you do?

Negotiating Skills

1. If I told you I was only going to give you a 5 percent pay raise, but you believed (based on current standards) you deserved 10 percent, what tactics would you use to convince me?

2. What was the toughest thing you have ever had to negotiate in your business career?

   a. What was the issue?

   b. What arguments did you make?

   c. What tactics did you employ?

   d. What was the end result?

Persuasiveness

1. Assume I have told you that I have interviewed three excellent candidates for this position, and you are

one of them. Convince me why you are the "best" candidate.

2. Give me an example where you failed to persuade someone to do something you felt would be good for business results.

   a. What was the issue?

   b. How did you attempt to persuade them?

   c. Why did your effort fail?

   d. What might you do differently today? Why?

Political Astuteness

1. What is your view of the role of politics in an organization?

2. Why do you feel this way?

3. What was the most difficult political decision you have had to make?

   a. What were the sensitivities?

   b. What were the risks?

   c. What factors needed to be considered, and why?

   d. What tact did you elect to take?

   e. What was the result?

Ability to Learn

1. What kinds of things do you learn quickly?

2. What kinds of things do you find difficult to learn?

3. Tell me about a situation that required you to learn something difficult.

   a. Why was it difficult to learn?

   b. What did you have to do to learn it?

   c. How long did it take?

   d. What was the end result?

Teamwork

1. What has been your experience in working as part of a team?

2. What do you see as being the advantages and disadvantages of working as part of a team? Why?

3. Give me an example of your involvement in a successful team effort.

   a. What role did you play?

   b. Why was the effort successful?

4. Give me an example of your involvement in a team effort that failed.

   a. What role did you play?

   b. What factors led to the failure?

CHAPTER 8 *The Interview*

You have now completed the "interview design" phase of the interviewing and selection process. At this point, you are well equipped to tackle the task at hand—selecting high performers. You are armed with the two main ingredients absolutely critical to choosing high performers. These are:

1. *High-Performance (Predictive) Model.* A well-defined model depicting the knowledge, skills, traits, characteristics, and behaviors known to be critical to high performance of the target position you are filling.

2. *Interview Plan.* A detailed interview design consisting of behaviorally based interview questions to systematically measure prospective candidates against the high-performance, predictive model.

As the strategic selection model (see Figure 8.1) shows, we are now ready for the interview itself. This chapter, then, will cover all aspects of conducting an effective interview discussion, including the basic preparation steps to set the stage for this important process.

THE INTERVIEW TEAM

The first step in preparing for an effective interview meeting is the selection and briefing of the interview team. Since the

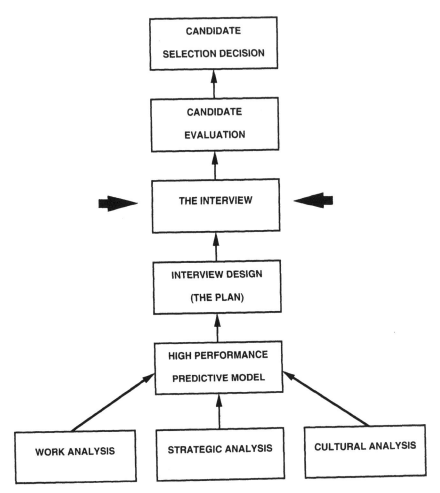

Figure 8.1 *Strategic Selection Model*

team is going to play a key role in the selection process, it is important for them to be familiar with the high-performance, predictive model and have a full appreciation for the selection criteria that will be used during the interview process. You can do this during an interview briefing meeting.

Selection of the interview team can often be critical to the organization's ability to accurately access prospective candidates. You must therefore be careful to select team members who are the most knowledgeable about the areas to be evaluated. This is especially true when measuring the candidate's job and strategic knowledge.

If you will be measuring candidate know-how in a position that requires highly technical or specialized knowledge, it is critical to the success of the selection process to have one or more team members who are technically qualified in the specialized area that you are attempting to measure.

If no such person exists within the organization, you may want to pull in an outside expert who has the knowledge to make a proper evaluation. Perhaps you can find a consultant who specializes in the field, or a knowledgeable technical person from a vendor organization. In fact, you will also likely need this person's help in designing the job, project, and strategic problems that you will use to evaluate the candidate's knowledge and qualifications to perform the technical aspects of the job.

In any event, you *must* have a qualified technical person on the team if you want to be sure that you are hiring someone who is truly capable of solving the key functional, project, and strategic problems for which this position is responsible. If you fail to satisfy this requirement, the cost of your hiring mistake could well run into the thousands, if not millions, of dollars.

Since a good part of what you will be measuring, beyond the candidate's technical fit, is cultural fit, where possible, it is a good idea to include team members from the immediate work group, who have firsthand knowledge of the organization's culture. They are likely to be far better qualified to judge the candidate's qualifications in this important arena than others who are less familiar with the cultural setting in which the work will be performed.

Finally, you will need to assign accountability to the team members for different aspects of the interview discussion. I recommend the use of group interviews, where the entire interview team meets with the candidate simultaneously, with one individual assigned the principal accountability for asking the interview questions and the balance of the team having responsibility for observing the candidate's behavior and taking careful notes.

This group interview meeting should be augmented by some quality one-on-one time with the hiring manager to whom the candidate will be reporting. This then allows the hiring manager to answer the many questions the candidate may have about a host of subjects important to his or her employment decision.

Use your interview team meeting to distribute and review the following important interview documents:

1. Memorandum explaining each team member's responsibility.
2. Schedule of the interview day including times, events, and participants.
3. Copy of the high-performance, predictive model.
4. Copy of the interview plan.
5. Copy of the candidate evaluation form.
6. Copy of the candidate's completed employment application form.
7. Copy of the candidate's resume.

Answer any questions from team members concerning their roles or the overall process for conducting the interview.

THE SETTING

The interview setting should be selected with the candidate's physical comfort and privacy as prime considerations. Avoid busy office areas where there is the temptation to allow the interview discussion to be interrupted by phone calls or questions from other employees. Nothing is more disconcerting and distracting to an otherwise good selection process than continuous interruptions.

Take the phone off the hook and instruct your secretary or administrative assistant that you are not to be interrupted during the interview discussion. Make sure there is adequate lighting and ventilation as well as comfortable seating. Have some coffee available and make sure the candidate will not be seated with the sun glaring in his or her eyes or will be subject to some other physically distracting or unpleasant condition.

Choose a conference room that is an appropriate size for the meeting—not too big or too small. Avoid cavernous rooms where people will be separated by a good distance and voices will echo off the empty walls. Wherever possible, choose a round table rather than a rectangle or a square one. This is far more conducive to creating an informal tone that will facilitate an open and friendly discussion.

APPLICATION FORM AND RESUME REVIEW

An important step in preparing for the interview discussion is the careful review of the two basic candidate documents—the employment application and the resume. Unfortunately, in too many cases, managers wait until the candidate arrives and then proceed to hurriedly review these important documents while the candidate patiently (or impatiently) waits for the interview to start.

Good interview planning requires that these documents be reviewed well in advance of the interview day. This can save considerable time and make the interview discussion far more informative and effective.

Many questions about the candidate's basic qualifications can be answered by reviewing these documents in advance. Thus, precious interview time can be saved and better utilized in exploring those qualifications that are not already evident from the resume and application form. Additionally, the candidate will have a far more favorable impression if you and the other team members have reviewed these documents in advance and are well prepared for the interview.

PREPARING TO SELL

An important aspect of interview preparation is preparing your "sales presentation." If your recruiting process turns up a really good prospect, you will need to be prepared to convince them of the many good reasons to join your team. Selling a good candidate cannot be left to chance.

Here are some important questions to consider when preparing your marketing strategy and presentation to the candidate:

1. What is unique or different about the work the candidate would be doing that most candidates would see as stimulating?

2. What is unique or different about your work environment that most good candidates would see as particularly positive?

3. What are you prepared to say concerning your commitment to personal training and career development?

4. What kind of favorable picture can you paint concerning opportunities for career advancement?

    a. What are the career avenues and options?

    b. What does it take to advance in this organization?

    c. Can you cite examples of others who have worked under you and experienced excellent advancement?

5. How will you describe the following items in the most favorable terms?

    a. The "performance evaluation process" (how people are evaluated and recognized for their contributions).

    b. The "salary administration program" (how employees are treated and rewarded financially for their contributions).

    c. The benefits program (uniqueness, distinctiveness).

If you want to convince high performers to come aboard and join your team, be particularly sensitive to any areas (see preceding questions) where you might be less competitive or particularly vulnerable. Decide what you are going to say about these areas in advance, rather than fumbling through them when confronted by the candidate during the interview. Think of ways you can put the most positive spin on these descriptions.

Finally, be sure that your interview plan has a strategy for "qualifying" the candidate. Any good salesperson knows that to make the sale, you must understand what will motivate your prospect to buy. The process used for defining these motivational factors is what is referred to as "qualifying the buyer." You must, therefore, determine what will motivate the candidate to leave his or her current position and join your organization.

Strategically, these motivational factors normally fall into two categories: "pushing" factors and "pulling" factors. The pushing factors are those elements of the candidate's current job or work environment with which he or she is not totally satisfied. These factors are pushing the candidate away from that employer and causing him or her to look elsewhere. The pulling factors, on the other hand (as you might guess), are those elements of your job opening and work environment that the candidate sees as attractive. These factors are pulling that candidate toward employment with your organization.

It is wise to establish both of these factors early in the interview discussion (or perhaps during an initial telephone screen of the candidate before the on-site interview) by asking one or more of the following questions:

1. To Establish Pushing Factors
   a. Linda, obviously if you were totally satisfied at the Hilton Company, we wouldn't be talking here today. What are some of the factors in your current work situation with which you are not completely satisfied? Why are these important to you?
   b. David, what are some of the factors you would hope to find in a new employment situation that are not present in your current work situation, and why are these important to you?

2. To Establish Pulling Factors
   a. Donna, what are some of the factors that motivated you to come and talk with us today? What did you find attractive?
   b. What was there about the description of our opportunity here at Wilson Company that sounded appealing to you?

Answers to both the pushing and pulling factors will provide you with some great material for crafting an effective marketing strategy. You now know what is important to the candidate and can design your sales presentation to emphasize these factors, thereby substantially improving your chances of landing the high-performance candidate. You should ask these questions early in the interview discussion, however, so you will buy some time to put together a successful sales strategy.

These motivational factors also will come in handy later, when you make an employment offer. Any good offer strategy will include some discussion with the employment candidate that reinforces the idea that these important needs can be well met in your work environment. This adds a certain amount of additional value that the candidate should find quite appealing if he or she elects to accept your offer and join your organization.

As part of your sale, you will also want to have other information available on the day of the interview so that you can provide the candidate with extensive data on both the company and community. These should include such items as:

1. Copy of the job description.
2. Annual report.
3. Recent press releases (that say positive things about the company).
4. Product literature.
5. Copy of a recent company newspaper or other similar employee communications document (especially if there are appropriate articles that could help your cause).
6. Summary of company benefits.
7. Information on local community.
8. Housing information.

If an out-of-town candidate looks particularly promising, based on early telephone interviews, you may want to include a short tour of the area for a quick "look-see" on the interview day. It adds a special personal touch if you do this personally;

however, if your schedule does not permit this extra, you may want to enlist the services of a knowledgeable real estate agent.

In any event, there should be a reasonable attempt to remove any of the candidate's doubts and concerns about what the local community has to offer by giving him or her a brief glimpse through a personal tour. This also demonstrates a degree of sensitivity and concern for the personal needs of the candidate that is normally very much appreciated. The warm feelings generated by this kind of personal attention can go a long way toward getting the candidate to say yes when it's time to offer employment.

GREETING THE CANDIDATE

You know that old saying, "It's the little things that are important." Well, this is true in interviewing as well. The small things that you do during the interview all demonstrate your interest in, and concern for, the candidate. The message to the candidate says, "You are important to me." Since people like to feel that they are important and matter to others, this message will get you a lot of mileage when it comes time for the employment offer and the candidate begins to think about whether he or she would enjoy working for you. It is at just that time that those "warm feelings" will likely again return, and the candidate will feel more positively inclined.

One of those little things you can do to create this warmth is to go to the lobby to greet the candidate personally. This friendliness and congeniality will encourage the candidate to feel that you care and that you are not a formal, stuffy individual who likes to maintain distance from subordinates. It will also help to set a more relaxed, informal tone for the interview that is conducive to having a free and open interchange of information—exactly what you want to have happen in the interview discussion.

Before going to the conference room, it is probably a good idea to take the candidate to your office for 10 or 15 minutes in preparation for the interview day. Offer the candidate a cup of coffee and take a few minutes to explain what is to take place. Provide the candidate with a copy of the interview schedule and go over the names and relationships of the interview team participants so the interviewee will know what to expect and who will be present.

Explain that the interview team will be meeting with the candidate as a group, but following this discussion you will have some one-on-one time together back here at your office, when you can answer the many questions that he or she may have about the particulars of the job and/or the company. Provide some explanation about how the team interview process will be conducted so there will be "no surprises."

This premeeting sets the stage for the formal interview, and puts the candidate at ease about what is going to happen. Typically, this informative discussion will relieve some of a candidate's anxiety and give the person a greater sense of expectation and control. Thus, the candidate will be more relaxed and natural, which is far more conducive to an effective and open interview discussion than if the candidate is anxiety ridden and "uptight." This more relaxed state will also give you a more accurate reading about what the candidate is typically like in the daily work environment, which is important in making accurate observations about his or her normal, everyday behavior.

Following this brief premeeting, you will then want to escort the candidate to the conference room, where the rest of the interview team is waiting. Make the appropriate introductions, offer some more coffee, and allow a couple of minutes for the candidate to get settled in with some small talk with the other members of the group. Once the candidate is comfortable, it is time for the interview introduction.

INTRODUCTORY STATEMENT

In the group interview setting, it is common for one group member to manage the interview process and ask the interview questions (following the interview plan). Traditionally, this same person sets the stage for the interview through a brief, but carefully worded introductory statement.

Such an introductory statement to frame the interview might go as follows:

> *Joe, we really appreciate your joining us here this morning and the interest you have expressed in our opportunity. Our review of your background indicates that you have some interesting qualifications and we are looking forward to our discussion.*
>
> *As you know, Joe, we will be talking to you about the position of Corporate Accounting Manager. This position, as you know, reports to me and is accountable for (brief description of principal duties) . . .*
>
> *Joe, since we are talking about an important career move for you and a key management position for us here at Baxter Corporation, it is important for both of us to be as open and straightforward with one another as possible. We are going to want to know as much as possible about your education, work experience, knowledge, skills, and overall capabilities for the type of work we offer. Likewise, you will want to know about the job, our work environment, career opportunities, and other items that will be important to your making a good career decision.*
>
> *Through an open sharing of information, we can jointly determine whether this will be a good fit for both of us. Being a good fit, of course, is of great importance to your professional satisfaction and overall career happiness. Likewise, a good fit will mean we have a satisfied and productive employee. So, let's be as open and candid as possible in our discussions with one another.*

Joe, I'd like to begin our discussion by learning more about your educational background. Tell me about (begin interview with first question from your interview plan) . . .

This kind of introduction tends to put both the company and the candidate on an equal footing. Both have an equal amount to gain (or lose) from the employment decision, so it stresses the importance of openness and frankness of the interview discussion. By positioning the interview in this way, the candidate can see the value to be gained by being open and disclosing. This is a nice way of reminding the candidate of the dangers of overselling and accepting a position that is an inappropriate match. The result is typically for the candidate to be more natural and avoid the temptation to overstate his or her abilities— from which nobody gains.

Additionally, explaining the basic focus of the interview process as well as the topics to be covered, tends to frame the interview. Again, this helps to alleviate some candidate anxiety by helping the person better anticipate what lies ahead.

OBSERVATION AND NOTE TAKING

The principal role of the interview team is threefold:

1. To observe the candidate's behavior.
2. To record these observations through effective note taking.
3. To ask follow-up questions for the purpose of gaining further clarity concerning the candidate's qualifications in those areas critical to successful job performance.

Since the interview design is already pretty much locked in place, the whole focus of the interview now needs to be in measuring whether or not the candidate has the qualifications to perform the job successfully. The interview plan that you have constructed will serve its purpose by keeping the interview team focused on those qualifications known to be required for job success. So, it is now time for careful listening, behavioral observation, and some careful note taking. In this way, candidate responses and behaviors can be accurately recalled when it is time for evaluation and the final employment decision.

Thus, the interview process at this point, calls for systematic execution of the interview plan (so painstakingly constructed in Chapter 6) and collection of the behavioral evidence that demonstrates the candidate's ability (or inability) to successfully satisfy the demands of the job (as defined by your high-performance, predictive model). During this note taking and observation phase, you will want to pay particular attention to the behavioral aspects of the candidate's answers (what the candidate has either "done" or "would do"). As you will recall from Chapter 3, "the best known predictor of future performance (or behavior) is current (or past) behavior in performing the same or similar kinds of work."

As each key selection factor from the interview plan is systematically explored during the interview discussion, therefore, you will want to take very careful notes about what the candidate actually "do" (or has done). This will begin to provide you with the cumulative behavioral evidence so critical to accurately predicting how the candidate will perform in the target position.

For an effective interview process, it is imperative that you not telegraph your desired answers to the interview questions. Following a candidate's answer to a given question, therefore, it is best not to comment on whether you "agree" or "disagree" with the candidate's response. Instead, simply move on to the next question. Your statement of agreement or disagreement will telegraph your position on certain key issues, thus biasing answers to future questions. The candidate will then begin to tell you what he or she feels you "want to hear" rather than what the person really believes. This will distort the behavioral evidence you are collecting throughout the interview process and result in an inaccurate profile.

Likewise, you should guard against nonverbal clues that will also telegraph your views to the candidate. Such things as nodding your head (either yes or no) or smiling in response to an answer will be duly noted and will begin to bias the candidate's answers to future questions. So, simply take appropriate notes and follow the interview plan by moving on to the next question, without in any way signaling either your approval or disapproval of the previous response. In this way you will have a far more reliable picture of what the candidate is really like.

CLOSING THE INTERVIEW

Once the interview plan has been exhausted and there are no further questions or situations to be posed to the candidate, it is time for the "interview close." At this point it is a good idea to change the scenery. So, you might want to leave the conference room and return, with the candidate, to the privacy of your office to close the interview.

Prior to beginning the actual close, you will first want to take time to answer specific questions the candidate may have concerning the opportunity. Depending on your level of interest in the candidate, you may also want to market your employment opportunity by activating the sales strategy that you formulated before the interview.

I strongly recommend that you reserve your selling strategy until the later stages of the interview discussion for two good reasons:

1. You don't want to bias the candidate's answers to your interview questions.
2. You don't want to waste valuable time selling a candidate in whom you have little or no interest.

If you position the "sale" at or near the beginning of the interview and the candidate becomes excited about the opportunity, there is a much higher probability that you will prejudice answers to the interview questions. Under these circumstances, the person is far more likely to say what he or she thinks you want to hear, rather than what he or she really thinks. Thus, you will not get a very accurate picture of the candidate's real feelings and behavior. Consequently, you will likely misjudge the candidate, substantially increasing the likelihood of a poor (and costly) hiring decision.

If, at the conclusion of the group interview you determine that you have further interest in the candidate, it is an excellent strategy for you to request feedback concerning the candidate's level of interest in your position. This can be done with a statement like the following:

Tim, now that you've had the chance to meet some of our people and discuss the position in some detail, I was wondering how you feel about this opportunity. Is this something that is of interest to you?

Provide an opportunity for the candidate to respond, and then say something to this effect:

As you view this opportunity, Tim, what aspects sound particularly interesting to you?

Allow time for response, and then follow with:

As you think about your criteria for making a good career decision, Tim, what, if any, aspects of our specific employment opportunity here at Mifflin Company are of concern to you?

This is excellent strategy from a marketing standpoint. Answers to the first question will provide you with some pretty good clues about what to reinforce and emphasize during the subsequent conversation when making the actual employment offer. Answers to the second question, in turn, will help you identify the barriers to getting an acceptance of your employment offer. Identifying these barriers, in advance of the employment offer, allows you the luxury of developing an effective strategy to counter them before they become an issue and the candidate declines your offer.

Unfortunately, hiring managers too often neglect getting this kind of feedback from candidates at the close of the interview discussion. Consequently, they are caught by surprise when the candidate declines the employment offer because of these barriers, at which time it is simply too late. So, use the interview close to collect this valuable information in advance of the employment offer, and then structure your offer strategy accordingly.

Where you know, at the time of the interview close, that the interview has gone well and there is a high probability that an employment offer will be forthcoming, provide the candidate with some positive feedback and express your interest in his or her employment candidacy. You can do this with a statement similar to the following:

Donna, although we have not yet had an opportunity to meet as an interview team and arrive at a final decision concerning your employment candidacy, I did want to let you know that I am personally very impressed with what I have seen. You appear to have much of what I am looking for, and I feel you could make a real contribution here at Wilson Company. I am anxious to talk with the other members of the team and look forward to getting back to you very shortly.

The timing and spontaneity of this positive feedback during the interview close will create some warm feelings on the part of the candidate. This delivers a very positive message to the candidate at a time when it will have maximum positive impact.

The same message coming a few days later (at the time of the employment offer) has much less overall impact. It may suggest to the candidate that the response to his or her candidacy was less than unanimous, and perhaps there was a lot of discussion about the pros and cons of making the employment offer. This expression of interest will simply not generate the same degree of positive feelings about the opportunity as would have resulted on the day of the interview. In this case, there is something to be said for spontaneity.

Last, but not least, show basic courtesy to the candidate by expressing appreciation for the visit:

Listen Jane, thanks very much for coming in to visit with us today. We appreciated the opportunity to talk with you and look forward to getting back to you shortly. Have a safe trip home!

Once again, a little sensitivity and courtesy can go a long way to leaving a favorable impression with the candidate.

Finally, take the time to personally see the candidate to the door and on their way. This little extra bit of personal attention and interest will not go unnoticed!

Well, now that the interview is over, it is time to review our notes and the data we have collected and arrive at an employment decision.

Candidate Evaluation

$\mathcal{T}$he next step in the strategic selection process (see Figure 9.1) is candidate evaluation. Candidate evaluation, by definition, is the process by which we compare the qualifications of the candidate with the requirements of the target position for the purpose of making a "hire" or "no hire" decision. More specifically, it is the process we use to compare the behavioral evidence collected during the interview discussion with the high-performance model (constructed in Chapter 6) as the basis for predicting whether or not the person we are considering for employment will be a high performer.

The focal point of this comparison is the candidate evaluation form, a document that, if well-designed, focuses our attention on the critical selection factors important to high performance of the job. So, as the first step in the candidate evaluation process we need to examine the candidate evaluation form and understand how it is to be used to evaluate prospective employees.

A recommended evaluation form is provided at the end of this chapter (page 183) for your reference. Take a few moments now to study and familiarize yourself with this form.

In Chapter 8, we recommended that the candidate evaluation form be standard issue to all members of the interview team prior to the interview discussions with employment candidates. Obviously, the intent of providing this document was to have the team members complete the form immediately following interview discussions, while information about the candidate is still fresh in their minds.

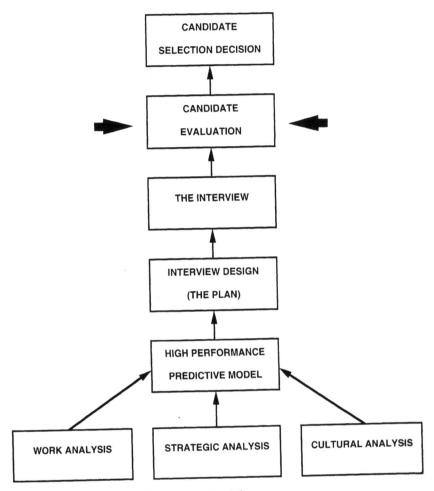

Figure 9.1   *Strategic Selection Model*

THE EVALUATION FORM

As you might suspect, review of the recommended candidate evaluation form will reveal that its design is centered on the high-performance, predictive model in Chapter 6. The logic of this design is inescapable. Since the predictive model reflects the qualifications required for high performance of the target position, it should stand to reason these same factors should be used as the basis for candidate evaluation and selection.

Therefore, the components of the evaluation form mirror the high-performance model and include the following:

1. Job knowledge (the knowledge required for performance of the core job).

2. Project knowledge (the knowledge needed to meet the special project responsibilities of the position).

3. Strategic knowledge (the knowledge required to drive strategic changes and support the long-term strategic goals of the organization).

4. Motivation to perform the type of work offered.

5. Organizational compatibility to include two key dimensions:

   a. Compatibility with work environment.

   b. Compatibility with high-performer profile.

This form thus provides a vehicle for systematically collecting all relevant candidate information to facilitate a focused and efficient employment selection process.

Let's now examine how this form is to be used in the interview and selection process.

ASSIGNING WEIGHTING FACTORS

Prior to beginning interviews, you will want to first determine the relative importance (or weighting) of the selection criteria against which the candidate's qualifications are to be measured using the following scale:

Weighting Factor	*Definition of Factor*
3	= *Critical* to Successful Job Performance
2	= *Important* to Successful Job Performance
1	= *Helpful* to Successful Job Performance

Certain qualifications are of greater importance than others in the performance of any job. Therefore, they should not receive the same weighting for candidate evaluation and selection purposes. By evaluating the degree of impact of each selection factor (contained on the candidate evaluation form) on the end results required of the job, it should be fairly easy for you to assign a relative weighting for each.

The preceding weighting scale appears in the upper right hand corner of the candidate evaluation form for ease of reference. A "weighting factor" box has also been provided on the evaluation form adjacent to each candidate selection factor. Use these boxes to record your numerical rating of each of the candidate selection criterion, based on its importance to successful job performance. Therefore, record a "3" if you deem the factor "critical" to successful performance, a "2" if considered "important" to successful performance, and a "1" if you feel the factor is "helpful" to job performance success.

You will note that the candidate evaluation form also provides "interview rating" boxes to record your rating of the candidate's qualifications (based on the scale provided) for each of the selection factors on the form. When this interview rating is multiplied by the weighted factor, a total rating is determined for each selection factor on the form.

INTERVIEW RATING

Immediately after the candidate interview, while details are fresh in mind, the members of the interview team should record their interview ratings in the boxes provided for this purpose on the evaluation form. Additionally, a few brief notes supporting these ratings should be recorded in the space provided for this purpose after each factor.

The interview scale for rating each of the candidate selection factors is as follows:

Rating		*Rating Definition*
3	=	Expert/Excellent Match
2	=	High/Good Match
1	=	Satisfactory/Acceptable
0	=	Unsatisfactory

TOTAL RATING

After all selection factors have been assigned an interview rating, the next step in the candidate evaluation process is to multiply the interview rating by the weighted factor to arrive at a total rating for each of the candidate evaluation factors on the candidate evaluation form. Adding these total ratings for the individual evaluation factors results in an "actual total rating," or score for the candidate under evaluation.

To complete the evaluation, you then need to calculate the "possible total rating" by multiplying the weighted factor assigned to each selection factor times 3 (the highest possible interview rating) to arrive at the highest possible total rating for each selection factor. Adding all these ratings together results in the "possible total rating."

Dividing the actual total rating (given the candidate) by the possible total rating (for the job) expresses the candidate's evaluation as a percentage of the total possible points. This percentage then provides a convenient way to numerically compare various candidates for the position in an effort to arrive at selection of the most qualified candidate. Thus a candidate who scored 90 percent (90 percent of the total possible points for the position) is clearly the preferred candidate over someone who scored only 75 percent. Likewise, someone who scores above the 90 percent level is a candidate who falls close to the high-performance model, and there is therefore an excellent chance that this candidate will prove to be a highly effective, productive employee.

Someone who scored 0 (unsatisfactory) on *any* candidate selection factor with a weighted factor of 3 (critical) is likely to be a poor risk for the position. Such a rating tells us that the individual is unable to perform at a satisfactory level in a key factor that is critical to successful job performance.

So, the use of the candidate evaluation form presented in this chapter has the following key advantages:

1. It is based on the high-performance, predictive model for the position (substantially enhancing the probability of selection of high-performing employees).

2. It focuses the evaluation on those factors that are "known" to be important to high performance.

3. It provides a consistent basis or standard against which *all* candidates are consistently rated (criteria are not left up to the whims of each interview team member to decide).

4. It allows for quantitative differentiation of selection criteria, by assigning higher weighted values to those selection factors known to have the greatest impact on successful job performance.

5. The use of quantitative overall ratings facilitates more accurate candidate comparison, increasing the probability of hiring the "best" qualified candidate. (This

would be a far more complex and less objective task than if a nonquantitative system were utilized.)

6. The use of the "percent of total possible" rating provides a more measurable, objective standard for determining a candidate's level of overall fit for the target position.

7. Quantitative ratings provide an excellent basis for comparing interview results across the team, focusing team discussion on major ratings discrepancies that might otherwise go unnoticed. (As will be discussed in the next chapter, such comparisons can improve the overall accuracy of the selection decision as well as serve as the basis for upgrading the evaluation and selection process.)

All of these advantages seem to strongly recommend the use of this type of evaluation approach over standard, nonquantitative methods of candidate evaluation.

OVERALL SUMMARY AND
EMPLOYMENT RECOMMENDATION

Page 8 of the candidate evaluation form provides for a summary of the overall strengths and shortcomings of the candidate along with a recommendation to either "hire" or "not hire." Here again, the quantitative ratings assigned to each selection factor by individual members of the interview team allow for quick and efficient identification of the candidate's key strengths and weaknesses. This greatly facilitates the writing of this summary and provides an excellent basis for supporting the hiring recommendation.

Before leaving this subject of candidate evaluation and continuing on with the final employment decision (see Chapter 10), it is important to point out that this phase of the selection process (candidate evaluation) was based on use of an interview plan that is well grounded in behaviorally based interviewing techniques. This interview plan, if executed as it was designed, will provide excellent behavioral evidence of the candidate's qualifications in each of the selection areas known to be critical to high performance in the job.

Since the foundation of the candidate evaluation is behaviorally based, as supported by modern interview theory, you should have an accurate and reliable basis for predicting future behavior and thereby selecting employees who will demonstrate above-average performance, once they are employed by the firm.

The next chapter will deal with making the final employment decision.

CANDIDATE EVALUATION FORM

Candidate Name: _____
Interviewed By: _____
Date Interviewed: _____
Company: _____
Div/Dept: _____
Position: _____

WEIGHTING FACTORS:

3 = Critical
2 = Important
1 = Helpful

RATING SCALE:

3 = Expert/Excellent Match
2 = High /Good Match
1 = Satisfactory/Acceptable
0 = Unsatisfactory

JOB KNOWLEDGE: (Measure: Knowledge Depth/Breadth, Ability to Apply, Quality of Solution)

| | | INTERVIEW RATING | X | WEIGHTED FACTOR | = | TOTAL RATING |

Problem # 1 _____
_____
_____
_____
_____

$\square$ X $\square$ = $\square$

Problem # 2 _____
_____
_____
_____
_____

$\square$ X $\square$ = $\square$

Problem # 3 _____
_____
_____
_____
_____

$\square$ X $\square$ = $\square$

Problem # 4 _____
_____
_____
_____

$\square$ X $\square$ = $\square$

Candidate Name: _____

WEIGHTING
FACTORS:

3 = Critical
2 = Important
1 = Helpful

RATING SCALE:

3 = Expert/Excellent Match
2 = High /Good Match
1 = Satisfactory/Acceptable
0 = Unsatisfactory

JOB KNOWLEDGE (Continued)   (Measure: Knowledge Depth/Breadth, Ability to Apply, Quality of Solution)

	INTERVIEW RATING	X	WEIGHTED FACTOR	=	TOTAL RATING

Problem # 5 _____
_____
_____
_____
_____

☐ X ☐ = ☐

Problem # 6 _____
_____
_____
_____

☐ X ☐ = ☐

Problem # 7 _____
_____
_____
_____

☐ X ☐ = ☐

Problem # 8 _____
_____
_____
_____

☐ X ☐ = ☐

Candidate Name: _____

<u>**WEIGHTING FACTORS:**</u>

3 = **Critical**
2 = **Important**
1 = **Helpful**

<u>**RATING SCALE:**</u>

3 = **Expert/Excellent Match**
2 = **High /Good Match**
1 = **Satisfactory/Acceptable**
0 = **Unsatisfactory**

<u>PROJECT KNOWLEDGE:</u>   (Measure: Knowledge Depth/ Breath, Ability to Apply, Quality of Solution)

Problem # 1

INTERVIEW RATING   X   WEIGHTED FACTOR   =   TOTAL RATING

☐ X ☐ = ☐

Problem # 2

☐ X ☐ = ☐

Problem # 3

☐ X ☐ = ☐

Problem # 4

☐ X ☐ = ☐

Problem # 5

☐ X ☐ = ☐

Candidate Name: _____

<u>**WEIGHTING FACTORS:**</u>	<u>**RATING SCALE:**</u>
3 = Critical	3 = Expert/Excellent Match
2 = Important	2 = High /Good Match
1 = Helpful	1 = Satisfactory/Acceptable
	0 = Unsatisfactory

Problem # 6 _____

INTERVIEW RATING X WEIGHTED FACTOR = TOTAL RATING

□ X □ = □

<u>STRATEGIC KNOWLEDGE:</u>   (Measure: Knowledge Depth/ Breadth, Ability to Apply, Quality of Solution)

Problem/ Barrier # 1 _____

□ X □ = □

Problem/ Barrier # 2 _____

□ X □ = □

Problem/ Barrier # 3 _____

□ X □ = □

Problem/ Barrier # 4 _____

□ X □ = □

Candidate Name: _____

WEIGHTING FACTORS:

3 = Critical
2 = Important
1 = Helpful

RATING SCALE:

3 = Expert/Excellent Match
2 = High /Good Match
1 = Satisfactory/Acceptable
0 = Unsatisfactory

Problem/
Barrier # 5 _____
_____
_____
_____
_____

INTERVIEW RATING X WEIGHTED FACTOR = TOTAL RATING

☐ X ☐ = ☐

Problem/
Barrier # 6 _____
_____
_____
_____
_____

☐ X ☐ = ☐

MOTIVATION TO SOLVE KEY PROBLEMS: (Measure: Degree of Technical Challenge, Stimulation, & Motivation Based on Reaction to Past Jobs)

Observations _____
_____
_____
_____
_____

☐ X ☐ = ☐

ORGANIZATIONAL CULTURE (FIT):

A. WORK ENVIRONMENT: (Measure: Degree of Compatibility with Existing Environment)

1. General Work Environment: (Compatibility)

_____
_____
_____

☐ X ☐ = ☐

Page 5

Candidate Name: _____

<u>WEIGHTING FACTORS:</u>

3 = Critical
2 = Important
1 = Helpful

<u>RATING SCALE:</u>

3 = Expert/Excellent Match
2 = High /Good Match
1 = Satisfactory/Acceptable
0 = Unsatisfactory

A. <u>WORK ENVIRONMENT</u>: (Continued)   (Measure: Degree of Compatibility with Existing Environment)

	INTERVIEW RATING	X	WEIGHTED FACTOR	=	TOTAL RATING

2. <u>Type of Work</u>: (Compatibility)

_____
_____
_____

[ ] X [ ] = [ ]

3. <u>Decision-Making, Resource Allocation, Planning & Strategy Formulation</u>:

(Compatibility)

_____
_____
_____

[ ] X [ ] = [ ]

4. <u>Effective Working Relationships - External</u>: (Compatibility)

_____
_____
_____

[ ] X [ ] = [ ]

5. <u>Effective Working Relationships - Internal</u>: (Compatibility)

_____
_____
_____

[ ] X [ ] = [ ]

6. <u>Preferred Management Philosophy & Style</u>: (Compatibility)

_____
_____
_____

[ ] X [ ] = [ ]

Candidate Name: _____

<u>WEIGHTING</u>
<u>FACTORS</u>:

<u>RATING SCALE</u>:

3 = Critical
2 = Important
1 = Helpful

3 = Expert/Excellent Match
2 = High /Good Match
1 = Satisfactory/Acceptable
0 = Unsatisfactory

B. <u>PERSONAL PROFILE</u>: (Measure: Degree of Similarity with "High Performer" Profile)

1. <u>Personal Style - Traits, Characteristics & Behaviors</u>:
   (Comparison - "High Performer")

   INTERVIEW   WEIGHTED   TOTAL
   <u>RATING</u> X <u>FACTOR</u> = <u>RATING</u>

   [ ] X [ ] = [ ]

2. <u>Operating Style & Philosophy</u>: (Comparison - "High Performers")

   [ ] X [ ] = [ ]

3. <u>Management Style & Philosophy</u>: (Comparison - "High Performers")

   [ ] X [ ] = [ ]

4. <u>Business Philosophy</u>: (Comparison - "High Performers")

   [ ] X [ ] = [ ]

ACUTAL TOTAL RATING [ ]

POSSIBLE TOTAL RATING [ ]

% OF POSSIBLE TOTAL [ ]

Candidate Name: _____

STRENGTHS:

_____
_____
_____
_____
_____
_____
_____
_____

SHORTCOMINGS:

_____
_____
_____
_____
_____
_____
_____
_____
_____

RECOMMENDATION: (Check One)   **HIRE** ☐   **DO NOT HIRE** ☐

(WHY?)

_____
_____
_____
_____
_____

Candidate Selection Decision

*I*n the previous chapter, we focused on the topic of candidate evaluation, providing you with a process for systematically collecting information about the candidate's qualifications in those areas important to successful job performance. As confirmed by the strategic selection model that we have been following throughout this book (see Figure 10.1), the final step in the interviewing and selection process is the actual selection of the final candidate.

Importantly, the process that we have followed to arrive at this point has been based on the use of a high-performance model, a methodically prepared model representing the traits, characteristics, and qualifications known to be critical to performance of the target position at a high-performance level. This model is the standard against which prospective candidates are measured during the interview process to predict the probability of superior performance.

So far, we have used the high-performance, predictive model as the basis for interview design and the development of our final interview plan. The interview plan has been based on modern interview theory. It employs behaviorally based interview questions that allow us to use current or past behavior as the basis for predicting future behavior (how the candidate will behave or what the candidate will do once in the actual job). According to interview theory, this is the best, most reliable basis for selecting people who will be successful in the job.

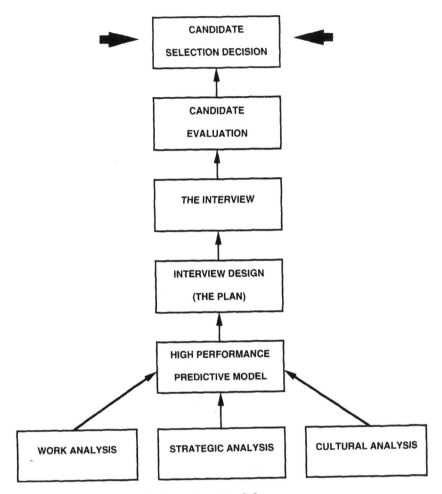

Figure 10.1 *Strategic Selection Model*

Finally, as already discussed, in the past chapter we showed you how to systematically collect and organize data, obtained from the interview discussions with the candidate, in an efficient manner making use of the candidate evaluation form. This form not only allowed us to collect relevant data to job performance but also provided the vehicle for assigning a quantitative interview rating to each of the selection factors known to be critical to successful job performance. Additionally, it also permitted us to weight each of the selection factors on the basis of its overall importance to successful performance of the target position. And finally, the evaluation form provided us with a means of assessing the overall worth of the candidate by assigning a total interview rating (also shown as a percentage of the total possible points or score that the interviewee could attain as a candidate for the target position).

The rest of this chapter deals with the subject of how to arrive at the selection or hiring decision. Specifically, "How do we take the data contained in the candidate evaluation form and use it to arrive at a decision to select (or not select) a given candidate?" This chapter will provide you with the process for accomplishing this goal.

TEAM REVIEW

Since we have thoroughly involved our interview team as an integral part of the candidate interview and evaluation process, it seems only fitting that we get the full benefit of the members' input before making the final selection decision. This is accomplished, following the interview, through a final meeting of the full interview team.

It is important to bring the team together as soon as possible after the interview. You'll want to tap into their information and observations about the candidate while this information is still fresh in their minds. It's difficult to remember much in terms of fine details a week or two after the interview event. For this reason, I strongly recommend that the final meeting of the interview team take place within a day or two of the actual interview date.

Each member of the team should complete and bring a copy of the candidate evaluation form to the meeting. This form will serve as the basis for discussions about the candidate as well as for critical input to the actual selection process.

TEAM EVALUATION FORM

To facilitate an orderly and efficient discussion among the team members, I recommend that you use a team evaluation form (see Figure 10.2). This form is arranged as a matrix, allowing the facilitator to record each team member's interview rating for the candidate selection factors evaluated during the interview. Additionally, space is provided for the meeting facilitator to record the total rating of each interview team member along with his or her hiring recommendation.

Once the ratings have been recorded, the facilitator encourages the team members' participation by systematically discussing each selection criterion against which the team evaluated the candidate. Where interview ratings are consistent and team members evaluated that factor at about the same level, probably not much discussion will be required. On the other hand, where there is a large discrepancy in a candidate's interview ratings (a difference of two or more levels in the rating scale), as assigned to a given selection factor by various team members, these rating differences must be thoroughly explored and reconciled before making a final selection decision.

Experience has shown that discrepancies of two levels or more on the rating scale may be caused by one of the following factors:

1. A difference in how team members perceived the candidate's level of qualification (for a given selection factor).

2. Lack of uniform definition or understanding of the selection criteria.

The purpose of the discussion is to determine what caused the large differential in ratings. A lack of understanding of the selection factor can be easily remedied through clarification of the intended meaning of the measurement standard. After arriving at a uniform definition, it is usually quite easy to reach accord on a uniform rating of the candidate on this factor,

SELECTION CRITERIA	WEIGHTED FACTOR	INTERVIEWER A RATING	INTERVIEWER B RATING	INTERVIEWER C RATING
JOB KNOWLEDGE				
PROBLEM 1				
PROBLEM 2				
PROBLEM 3				
PROBLEM 4				
PROBLEM 5				
PROBLEM 6				
PROBLEM 7				
PROBLEM 8				
PROJECT KNOWLEDGE				
PROBLEM 1				
PROBLEM 2				
PROBLEM 3				
PROBLEM 4				
PROBLEM 5				
PROBLEM 6				
STRATEGIC KNOWLEDGE				
PROBLEM 1				
PROBLEM 2				
PROBLEM 3				
PROBLEM 4				
PROBLEM 5				
PROBLEM 6				
MOTIVATION TO PERFORM				

(continued)

Figure 10.2   *Team Evaluation Form*

SELECTION CRITERIA	WEIGHTED FACTOR	INTERVIEWER A RATING	INTERVIEWER B RATING	INTERVIEWER C RATING
WORK ENVIRONMENT				
GENERAL WORK ENVIRONMENT				
TYPE OF WORK				
DECISION-MAKING, RESOURCE ALLOCATION, PLANNING & STRATEGY FORMULATION				
EFFECTIVE RELATIONSHIPS - EXTERNAL				
EFFECTIVE RELATIONSHIPS - INTERNAL				
MANAGEMENT PHILOS./STYLE				
PERSONAL PROFILE				
PERSONAL STYLE				
OPERATING STYLE				
MANAGE. STYLE				
BUSINESS PHILOSOPHY				
ACTUAL TOTAL RATING				
POSSIBLE TOTAL RATING				
% OF POSSIBLE TOTAL				

Figure 10.2 *(continued)*

following a brief discussion of each team member's observations of the candidate based on the new, revised definition.

Where the culprit is not "selection factor definition" but, instead, is a genuine difference in the way various team members perceived the candidate's qualifications, the task is a little more daunting. Here, however, it is essential for the team to agree on the rating if the interests of good selection and organizational productivity are truly to be served. Failure to reach accord, in many cases, results in faulty employee selection along with the enormous financial (and other) penalties for the firm.

USE OF "BEHAVIORAL EVIDENCE"

At the root of many interview team rating discrepancies is that old nemesis—"perception." Each member looks through different glasses when perceiving the candidate's qualifications. Herein lies the basis for much of the employment discrimination in the United States.

It is the job of the meeting facilitator, in these circumstances, to cut through the perceptions of the various team members, and get to the reality of the candidate's qualifications. Team members must put aside their individual perceptions and focus on the "behavioral evidence" of the candidate's ability to perform in the selection area being scrutinized. The facilitator should ask the participants these questions:

1. What observed "behavior" supports a given interview rating level?

2. What did the candidate actually "do" or say he or she would "do" in that selection area, to support a given rating?

3. How did the candidate "perform" in this area in past jobs?

4. What "behavioral evidence" can be cited to support this level of past performance?

5. What problems were posed to the candidate in this area during the interview discussion, and what did the candidate "do" to address these problems.

Again, you need to refocus the interview team members on actual behavior as the basis for evaluating the candidate's qualifications. As we already know, this behavior is the most accurate predictor of job performance success, not the perceptions of the members of the interview team about the candidate's qualifications.

You are going to find that by focusing the group on behavioral evidence, most of these interview rating differences are going to disappear. Usually, after carefully recalling and reviewing the specific replies of the candidate, the group will be able to reconcile these rating differences, and arrive at a consensus. Where this is not the case and the selection factor under evaluation is critical to effective job performance, it is time to have some further discussion with the candidate on this topic before proceeding to a premature employment or selection decision. Perhaps this is also an area you will want to earmark as important for discussion during the candidate reference check process.

In any event, by the end of the interview team meeting, the team should reach a consensus on the candidate's interview ratings. This is particularly vital for any selection factors that have been categorized as "critical" or "important" to job performance success.

NO PERFECT CANDIDATES

I have been working in and or around the employment process as a professional for close to 30 years and have *never* been privileged to interview the "perfect candidate" (one who would score at the expert or excellent level in *all* selection factors important to job performance). Like free lunches, such candidates just don't exist!

If you ever come across what you believe to be the perfect candidate, then it is time to go back and examine either your selection criteria or your interview process (if not both). The best we can usually hope for is a candidate who ranks "high" in all the selection factors known to be critical to successful job performance.

So, when making the employee selection decision, you will be forced to select someone who is "less than ideal" to fill your position requirements. It is just a matter of where you can afford to make some compromises without seriously jeopardizing functional productivity and efficiency. This is where those weighted factors you assigned to each of the selection factors on the candidate evaluation form now come into play.

If you are intent on hiring high performers, it is imperative at this point, that you pay particular attention to those selection factors to which you assigned a weighting factor of 3. These are the factors that you have designated as critical to successful job performance. One key principle to remember is this:

Never hire a candidate who rates lower than expert/ excellent match (3) or high/good match (2) in any of the candidate selection factors rated as "critical" to successful job performance.

As soon as you compromise your standards and hire someone who ranks as either satisfactory (1) or unsatisfactory (0) in any dimension of the job judged critical to successful performance, you have jeopardized performance in one or more critical areas of the job. This, by definition, guarantees that you have hired someone who will turn in less than stellar performance! In doing so, you have already forgone the opportunity to hire a high performer who can perform at a superior level in *all* areas critical to job success.

Likewise, the second principle of high-performer selection is this:

> *Avoid selection of individuals who consistently score at the satisfactory (1) or unsatisfactory (0) rating level in those selection criteria rated as "important" to successful job performance.*

Although high performance will usually not suffer when the candidate scores high in the critical selection dimensions of the job, something less than high performance is likely to occur when there begins to be a pattern of either satisfactory or unsatisfactory ratings in areas important to successful job performance. It is time, then, to examine how many factors are affected and what the overall impact on job performance is likely to be.

RISK ANALYSIS

It is important to realize that in any employee selection process there are going to be certain tradeoffs. As stated previously, there is never going to be the perfect candidate (one who rates a "3" in all selection categories). So, to make an intelligent selection decision, you will need to do some risk analysis to ascertain the degree of exposure represented by these tradeoffs, prior to moving ahead with your final candidate selection decision. Here is where the weighted factors, you previously assigned to the selection criteria, can prove particularly helpful.

To assess the potential risks associated with any employee selection decision, it is suggested that you follow the following steps:

1. Review the candidate evaluation form for selection factors having a weighted factor of either 2 or 3—meaning they are either important or critical to successful job performance.

2. Determine in which of these key factors the candidate has been rated as satisfactory/acceptable (1) or unsatisfactory (0).

3. Answer the following questions with respect to each of these factors:

   a. What impact will this deficit have on overall job/department results?

   b. Will this create any major problems?

   c. What can be done, within a reasonable time frame, to develop and improve the candidate's qualifications in this deficit area?

   d. What other group members can provide temporary support until the candidate can come up to speed in this deficit area?

By approaching the analysis in this way, you are not ignoring those areas of job performance that will require added temporary support and some bolstering up. By putting an appropriate game plan in place and planning for the candidate's development in deficit areas, many times you can effectively meet the key job responsibilities and still minimize the risk of adverse exposure.

On the other hand, should your risk analysis lead you to conclude that the risks are too great, that no one is available to provide the necessary temporary support, or that the likelihood of training the candidate in a reasonable time frame is unrealistic, it is probably time to move on and continue your search for a candidate whose qualifications present a better match for the requirements of the target position.

Having successfully concluded the risk analysis process and determined that your prospective candidate is a "good bet" as a high performer for the job, a final step (*the reference check*) is necessary before you move on to making that all important employment offer.

THE REFERENCE CHECK

The days of the "tell me what you think of good old Joe" reference checks have gone the way of the dinosaur. To play a meaningful role in the selection process, the modern reference check must go well beyond this type of surface inquiry.

The reference check provides an excellent opportunity to confirm the behavioral observations made by the interview team during the interview process. Regardless of the excellence of the interview process, there is always the possibility that the candidate can fake answers to interview questions and behave differently than he or she might in the actual work environment. Enter the reference check!

It is pretty hard for a person to hide characteristics, traits, and abilities from people with whom he or she has worked for a while. These individuals have had plenty of opportunities to observe the employee's behavior in work-related circumstances over an extended period. Therefore, they are an important resource to tap prior to arriving at that final employment or selection decision.

When conducting a reference check, I recommend that employers check five to seven references in the following categories:

1. Current boss (where feasible).

2. Past bosses.

3. Peers in the same function.

4. Subordinates (if in management).

5. Internal customers or clients (when in a staff service function).

Discussing the candidate with this many references, who represent a variety of vantage points, will allow you to get a clear and accurate picture of the candidate's qualifications profile. If carefully designed, the reference check will confirm (or deny) the behavioral observations and conclusions of the interview process. It is an excellent tool, therefore, and deserves to be an important part of the selection process.

Because of various laws that protect the privacy of employees and their work records, many companies have strict policies requiring employees to channel all reference calls to the Human Resources department, where personnel will only provide minimal verification information such as dates of employment, job title, and compensation level. They are usually unwilling to provide additional information because of the potential for litigation.

Despite these strict policies prohibiting detailed information, I can assure you such references are a commonplace phenomenon in the everyday world of employment and selection. In fact, I have spent over 10 years in the retained search business and have concluded more than 200 employment search assignments; during that time, I have been successful in getting bona fide, in-depth reference information for all but one candidate.

Should you experience difficulty in securing quality references, explain to the candidate that you cannot make an employment offer without the benefit of these reference discussions. You will be surprised to learn how quickly things will shift, and you'll find yourself having in-depth discussions with the candidate's references during the evenings and weekends when they no longer feel the constraints of the corporate environment.

To protect yourself and the reference sources with whom you need to speak, you might want to consider requiring the candidate to sign a "hold harmless" agreement as a prelude to the reference checking process. Such a document would serve to hold both you and the reference sources "harmless" should the candidate not like the outcome of the reference checking process. Consult an attorney concerning the design and content of this agreement to be sure that you are on solid legal ground should you decide to use this approach.

The content of the reference check should closely parallel your interview plan design. The same basic topics need to be covered to ensure that the reference will validate the outcome of the interview process. Since the reference check is, by necessity, a much shorter discussion than the interview, it is important to effectively utilize time in measuring factors that are truly important to successful job performance.

The reference design should, where possible, include questions to probe the candidate's qualifications in all areas that have been assigned a weighted factor of 3 (critical to job performance success). After all, misjudging a candidate in any of these critical areas will surely spell disaster from a selection standpoint. Where time permits, move on to some of the selection areas to which you have assigned a weighted factor rating of 2 (important to successful job performance). Eventually, should the reference seem willing to talk further, move finally to the selection factors with a helpful (1) rating.

As with interview design, reference check design should not just seek the reference source's opinion but should strive to obtain behaviorally based evidence of candidate capability as well. Thus, ask for specific examples of things the candidate has done to support these perceptions and opinions. Be sure not to accept just surface remarks about the candidate's ability in a certain area. Use some of the interview techniques learned earlier in this book (see Chapter 4) to ask insightful, probing questions that reveal behavior and actual results. As a follow-up to a positive example of a given accomplishment, ask the reference, "In what ways might that result have been improved?"

Also, how you go about framing the reference check at the beginning of the discussion can often have a great deal of bearing on just how candid and accurate the reference source may be willing to be. Also, should the source seem reluctant to talk, you may wish to send him or her a copy of the hold harmless agreement the candidate has signed, which releases the source from any liability that might otherwise result from the discussion.

At the beginning of the discussion, you will want to emphasize to the reference source how important it is to the candidate that this be a good fit. Also, it is a good idea, early on, to verbalize that it will not be to the candidate's advantage to accept a position for which he or she is not particularly suited. Such decisions are usually short-lived and can have a major disruptive effect on the candidate's career. In such cases, both the candidate and company lose; nobody comes out a winner.

Since this kind of reminder is true, it has a sobering effect on the reference source and will generally cause the person to be concerned about presenting inaccurate or misleading information about the candidate. It creates a sense of shared responsibility in achieving an appropriate match between the employer and the prospective employee.

Here is an example of what you might say when framing the reference discussion:

Mr. Warren, David Henson has given me your name as a reference. As you may be aware, Morgan Company is considering David for the position of Cost Accounting Manager at our Waverly Division. In this position he will be responsible for managing a cost accounting department of 18 employees in a $33 million division that manufactures widgets (continue to provide brief description of principal duties and responsibilities).

Mr. Warren, this is an important position to us, and we want to be sure that David will be a good match for our requirements. It is equally important to David that this be a good match, since a poor decision on his part could prove disruptive at this stage of his career. I would appreciate, therefore, if you would be very open in sharing some important information about David's performance and qualifications with me. I know that this will be in David's best interests, as well as ours.

As you can see, this is a great way to position the reference discussion, since it stresses the value of accurate information to David as well as the employer. Under these circumstances, reference sources are far more prone to be candid and will often share information that they would not have previously disclosed.

Once you have concluded the reference checks, and compared the behavioral evidence with that collected during the interview process itself, you are far better prepared to make that all-important selection decision. By now, however, a good deal of the risk has been removed from the process, and there is a substantially improved likelihood that you will be able to pick those high performers who are so critical to the organization's competitive advantage and strategic success.

Index

If you're not looking here, you're hardly looking.

There are lots of publications you can turn to when you're looking for a job. But in today's tough job market, you need the National Business Employment Weekly. It not only lists hundreds of high-paying jobs available now at major corporations all across the country, it also gives you valuable strategies and advice to help you land one of those jobs. NBEW is a Wall Street Journal publication. It's the leading national job-search and career guidance publication and has been for over ten years. Pick it up at your newsstand today. Or get the next 12 issues delivered first class for just $52 by calling toll-free...

800-367-9600

National Business Employment Weekly

If you're not looking here, you're hardly looking.

22089388R00121

Made in the USA
Lexington, KY
11 April 2013